S

ALEXANDER POPE

An Annotated Bibliography, 1945-1967

ALEXANDER POPE

An Annotated Bibliography, 1945-1967

by

CECILIA L. LOPEZ, 1941-

UNIVERSITY OF FLORIDA PRESS

Gainesville

1970

A University of Florida Press Book

*Library of Congress
Catalog Card Number 78-99213*
ISBN 0-8130-0292-3

PRINTED BY
STORTER PRINTING COMPANY, INCORPORATED
GAINESVILLE, FLORIDA

PREFACE

IN 1945 JAMES EDWARD TOBIN published a bibliography of Popean criticism entitled *Alexander Pope: A List of Critical Studies Published from 1895 to 1944*. A complete bibliography on Pope has not appeared since Tobin's publication; therefore, it is the purpose of this bibliography to supplement Mr. Tobin's list. This work is an annotated bibliography of critical editions and works on Alexander Pope covering the years 1945 through 1967.

Every effort has been made to insure the completeness of the entries within this bibliography. I have annotated critical editions of Pope's poetry, prose, and correspondence as well as critical studies in scholarly journals and books. Foreign items and a few periodicals and books which were impossible to obtain are not annotated; these items are preceded by an asterisk.

Since Tobin's annotations are minimal, I have not followed his policy. I have endeavored to make the annotations as informative as possible so that this bibliography may be helpful to future investigators. Objectivity has been the criterion; value judgments have not been consciously attempted in the annotations.

Annotations are followed by references to reviews of books and articles where such references exist, particularly reviews that have been listed in the annual bibliography of *Philological Quarterly*. Cross references are included in annotations where reference is made to another item. The numbers refer to entry, not page, numbers.

A comprehensive index of topics, authors, and titles of Pope's works has been provided. In each instance, the number or numbers that follow the entries in the index refer to the numbered entries in the bibliography, not to the page numbers of the text. The author, authors, editor, or editors of every work listed, plus all persons mentioned within the annotations, have been indexed. Topical headings, as well as Pope's works, are listed alphabetically throughout the index. In addition, the

v

index provides a complete system of cross-references for the bibliography.

Special recognition is due to Dr. Sara Herndon, Professor of English, Florida State University. Her scholarship and genuine enthusiasm for the teaching of English literature have earned my respect and admiration. Dr. Herndon's cheerful suggestions, assistance, and criticism not only initiated this bibliography, but also made its completion possible.

January, 1969   CECILIA L. LOPEZ

ABBREVIATIONS

AN&Q	American Notes & Queries
Archiv	Archiv für das Studium der neueren Sprachen und Literaturen
BA	Books Abroad
BC	Book Collector
BNYPL	Bulletin of the New York Public Library
CE	College English
CentR	The Centennial Review of Arts and Sciences
CL	Comparative Literature
CLAJ	College Language Association Journal (Morgan State College, Baltimore)
CQR	Church Quarterly Review
CritQ	Critical Quarterly
DA	Dissertation Abstracts
DR	Dalhousie Review
DUJ	Durham University Journal
EA	Études anglaises
EIC	Essays in Criticism
ELH	Journal of English Literary History
ELN	English Language Notes
ES	English Studies
HLB	Harvard Library Bulletin
HLQ	Huntington Library Quarterly
HudR	Hudson Review
JEGP	Journal of English and Germanic Philology
KR	Kenyon Review
MCR	Melbourne Critical Review
MLJ	Modern Language Journal
MLN	[Modern Language Notes]
MLQ	Modern Language Quarterly
MLR	Modern Language Review
MP	Modern Philology
N&Q	Notes & Queries
NYHTBR	New York Herald Tribune Book Review
OED	Oxford English Dictionary
PBA	Proceedings of the British Academy
PBSA	Papers of the Bibliographical Society of America
PLL	Papers on Language and Literature
PMASAL	Papers of the Michigan Academy of Science, Arts, and Letters
PMLA	[Publications of the Modern Language Association of America]
PQ	Philological Quarterly
QQ	Queen's Quarterly
RECTR	Restoration and Eighteenth Century Theatre Research
REL	Review of English Literature
RES	Review of English Studies

SAQ	South Atlantic Quarterly
SatR	Saturday Review
SEL	Studies in English Literature, 1500-1900
SNL	Satire Newsletter (State University College, Oneonta, N.Y.)
SP	Studies in Philology
SR	Sewanee Review
SRL	Saturday Review of Literature
SWR	Southwest Review
TLS	Times (London) Literary Supplement
Thoth	Journal of the English Graduate Group, Department of English, Syracuse University
TSL	Tennessee Studies in Literature
TSLL	Texas Studies in Literature and Language
UKCR	University of Kansas City Review
UTQ	University of Toronto Quarterly
WHR	Western Humanities Review
WMQ	William and Mary Quarterly
YR	Yale Review

CONTENTS

INTRODUCTION / 1

CRITICAL EDITIONS / 4

BIBLIOGRAPHY / 9

MANUSCRIPTS / 10

BIOGRAPHY / 13

POPE AS A CRITIC / 20

POPE AS A SOURCE OR INFLUENCE / 24

EIGHTEENTH- AND NINETEENTH-CENTURY
CRITICISM OF POPE / 30

GENERAL CRITICISM / 38

STYLE: POETICAL TECHNIQUES / 58

PASTORALS AND *WINDSOR FOREST* / 71

ESSAY ON CRITICISM / 75

RAPE OF THE LOCK / 81

ELOISA TO ABELARD / 90

ESSAY ON MAN / 92

MORAL ESSAYS / 103

EPISTLE TO DR. ARBUTHNOT / 107

SATIRES / 109

DUNCIAD / 115

OTHER WRITINGS / 125

POPE AS A TRANSLATOR AND EDITOR / 132

CORRESPONDENCE / 138

ADDITIONAL FOREIGN CRITICISM / 144

INDEX / 145

INTRODUCTION

JAMES L. CLIFFORD'S discussion (entry 184) of contemporary scholarship on Pope, Swift, Boswell, and Johnson is a comprehensive analysis of the major trends. This introduction, therefore, limits itself to brief comments on some of the more important developments and needs in Popean scholarship since 1945.

A most important development in the past quarter of a century has been the publication of Pope's works in the valuable Twickenham Edition. Editors of the caliber of Maynard Mack, John Butt, and James Sutherland, to name a few, have not only insisted upon fastidious editing and accurate annotations and notes, but have also produced excellent introductions containing critical studies and analyses. This is also true of a few other texts, such as the *Moral Essays,* edited with an analytical introduction by James E. Wellington (21).

A major contribution to Popean scholarship is George Sherburn's *The Correspondence of Alexander Pope* (670). The meticulous editing that went into the production of this work is a significant example of the modern emphasis on conscientious scholarship and textual accuracy.

Although systematic analyses of Popean manuscripts are represented by the judicious scrutiny of critics like Robert M. Schmitz (330 and 355), Earl R. Wasserman (491), and Maynard Mack (36), only a relatively few essays have dealt with the problems of location and reproduction of manuscripts, areas in which there is still room for scholarly investigation. There is also an obvious need for an annotated bibliography on Pope starting with the late eighteenth century and continuing through 1945. Tobin's *List of Critical Studies* (26) is of limited value because it is not annotated and its inclusion of works is biased; it should be supplanted.

Perhaps the most serious area of neglect is that of critical biography. Numerous essays on specific biographical accounts such as Norman Ault's discussion of Pope's relationship with Addison (41), or Benjamin Boyce's description of Pope's friendship with Ralph Allen (45), or the many articles relating to Pope's estrangement from Lady Mary Wortley Montagu are available. However, no comprehensive biography has been published since George Sherburn's *Early Career of Alexander Pope*. A biography of Pope's later life, as unbiased, scholarly, and accurate as Sherburn's, is urgently needed.

Although not a major trend, the current enthusiasm for studies on Pope's garden and grotto at Twickenham should not be overlooked. Interesting essays on this topic have been written by such critics as Benjamin Boyce (44), Frederick Bracher (46), and Maynard Mack (61). Mack's essay is a good indication of the trend of this new focus on Pope's estate. Not only are the biographical and historical aspects of the garden and grotto examined, but their relationship and contribution to Pope's poetic sensibility, taste, and personality are studied. And of related biographical interest is William Kurtz Wimsatt, Jr.'s extensive work on the portraiture of Pope (74), certainly a long-neglected phase of Pope biography.

Much consideration has also been given to the influence and popularity of Pope's poetry in such countries as America, France, Germany, Iceland, Italy, and Spain. Most representative of these essays is Agnes Marie Sibley's *Alexander Pope's Prestige in America* (159).

Another general area of focus has been on inquiries into the major critical attitudes toward Pope in the eighteenth and nineteenth centuries. This emphasis on an objective assessment of Pope's literary reputation has produced some very interesting studies, one of which is Upali Amarasinghe's *Dryden and Pope in the Early Nineteenth Century. A Study of Changing Literary Taste, 1800-1830* (126).

Certainly the most impressive and important trend that is observable is the total reassessment of Pope, as a man and as a poet, that had occurred even before the 1940's. Critics such as James L. Clifford (see p. 119 of entry 184) generally point to the 1938 publications of Robert Kilburn Root's *The Poetical Career of Alexander Pope* and Geoffrey Tillotson's *On the Poetry of Pope* as the vanguards of this reassessment. Both men, as well as numerous other critics, consider Pope's verse as an intricate collage of ideas, theories, and poetical devices; consequently, they have helped to transform the sterotype of the "wicked wasp" who wrote epigrammatical prose into the image of a man whose poetry is prodigious.

Many such outstanding critics as Butt, Mack, Root, Sherburn, Tillotson, and Williams have greatly helped to effect the Pope revival. And another possible basis for this reassessment of Pope's poetry has been the past general acceptance of the procedures of the New Critics with their insistence on simple explication and de-emphasis of historical documentation.

But the scholarship of the 1960's is an apparent synthesis of the techniques of the New Critics with objective critical principles which include biographical and historical studies and analyses of basic themes, metaphor, imagery, allusion, tension, satire, mock-heroic stance, rhetorical structures, and devices such as the persona or the implied dramatic speaker. Excellent examples of the latter are Rebecca Price Parkin's *The Poetic Workmanship of Alexander Pope* (297) and Maynard Mack's "The Muse of Satire" (294).

The concentration of studies on the multiplicity of devices employed by Pope to achieve subtle effects and a variety of levels of meaning has established as fact the artistry of Pope's poetry. An inkling of the fervor of this new evaluation is especially prominent in the forty-four *Essential Articles for the Study of Alexander Pope* compiled by Maynard Mack (219). Even a cursory examination will substantiate the conclusion of modern thinkers that Pope was a sensitive human being and a fascinatingly complex poet.

CRITICAL EDITIONS

1. Audra, E., and Williams, Aubrey L. (eds.). *Pastoral Poetry and An Essay on Criticism.* Twickenham Edition of the Poems of Alexander Pope, vol. I. London: Methuen, 1961.

> Reprints the text of the Preface to *Works* (1717), *Discourse on Pastoral Poetry, Pastorals, Messiah, Windsor Forest, Essay on Criticism,* and various translations. Each text (exclusive of the Preface) is preceded by a history of the text and by a general criticism of the work. See also 176 and 200.

> Reviewed by Reginald L. Brett, *CritQ,* III (1961), 370–71; *TLS,* December 29, 1961, p. 930; Earl R. Wasserman, *PQ,* XLI (1962), 615–22; G. K. Hunter, *MLR,* LVII (1962), 595–96; Jacques Golliet, *EA,* XVI (1963), 84; Robert W. Rogers, *JEGP,* LXII (1963), 400–402; Rachel Trickett, *RES,* n.s., XIV (1963), 200–205; Bernhard Fabian, *Anglia,* LXXXI (1963), 250–56.

2. Ault, Norman, and Butt, John (eds.). *Minor Poems.* Twickenham Edition of the Poems of Alexander Pope, vol. VI. London: Methuen, 1954.

> Determines the canon of Pope's minor poems, arranges the poems in chronological order, appends a bibliography to each poem which specifies "the present position of autograph manuscripts and of contemporary transcripts" (p. xvi), provides "the history of the text of each poem" (p. xvii) in a footnote, and lists poems of doubtful authorship and of "poems wrongly attributed to Pope" (p. xvii).

> Reviewed by Alan Dugald McKillop, *PQ,* XXXIV (1955), 307–9; *TLS,* October 22, 1954, p. 672; Gwyn Jones, *MLR,* L (1955), 201; George Sherburn, *SR,* LXIII (1955), 330–37; Harold Williams, *RES,* n.s., VII (1956), 83–86.

3. Bateson, F. W. (ed.). *Epistles to Several Persons (Moral Essays).* Twickenham Edition of the Poems of Alexander Pope, vol. III, pt. 2. London: Methuen, 1951.

> Contains the texts of the following epistles: I (To Cobham), II (To a Lady), III (To Bathurst), IV (To Burlington), which are supplemented by detailed and interpretative foot-

notes and notes. The volume includes a critical introduction and the following appendices: "Who Was Atossa?" "Timon and the Duke of Chandos," and "A Master Key to Popery." A "Second Edition" appeared in 1961.

Reviewed by Gwyn Jones, *MLR*, XLVII (1952), 224–26; Harold Williams, *RES*, n.s., III (1952), 292–94; Robert W. Rogers, *PQ*, XXXI (1952), 285–87; Clarence Tracy, *QQ*, LVIII (1952), 448–50; *TLS*, June 1, 1951, p. 342.

4. Brady, Frank (ed.). *An Essay on Man.* Library of Liberal Arts. Indianapolis: Bobbs-Merrill, 1965.

Brady's introduction provides a brief discussion of the poem's ideas and structure.

5. Brockbank, Philip (ed.). *Selected Poems of Pope.* London: Hutchinson Educational, 1964.

Brockbank's selections are "represented by a number of complete poems, with only a token recognition of the longest pieces" (Preface). His introduction contains a general commentary on some of Pope's poetry.

6. *Brower, Reuben Arthur, and Bond, W. H. (eds.). *The Iliad.* New York: Macmillan, 1965.

7. *Butt, John (ed.). *Imitations of Horace.* Twickenham Edition of the Poems of Alexander Pope. London: Methuen, 1966.

8. ———. *Letters of Alexander Pope.* World's Classics, 574. London: Oxford University Press, 1960.

Butt's brief introduction considers the history of the publication of Pope's correspondence. For a fuller annotation see 661.

9. ———. *The Poems of Alexander Pope. A One-Volume Edition of the Twickenham Text with Selected Annotations.* New Haven: Yale University Press, 1963.

Contains in one volume "a reduced version of the Twickenham Edition" in six volumes. Butt includes "Pope's entire poetical work, except for the translations of Homer." Annotations and Pope's notes are included.

10. Cowler, Rosemary Elizabeth (ed.). "An Edition of the Prose Criticism of Alexander Pope." Unpublished Ph.D. dissertation, Yale University, 1956.

Provides extensive annotations and introductions to the texts of *Discourse on Pastoral Poetry; Guardian,* no. 40; Preface to *Iliad*; Postscript to *Odyssey*; Preface to *Works* (1717); Preface of Editor to *Shakespeare.* Cowler's annotations explore the extent to which Pope was derivative and provide an explication of the texts.

11. Davis, Herbert (ed.). *Alexander Pope: Poetical Works.* London: Oxford University Press, 1966.

Consists of the texts of all of Pope's poetical works except the translations of Homer. Three appendices provide *Rape of the Lock* (text of the first edition in two cantos); *A Character of Marlborough*; an extended version of *Essay on Man,* IV, 291–308; and the *Dunciad* (text of the first edition in three books).

12. Elwin, Rev. Whitwell, and Courthope, William J. (eds.). *The Works of Alexander Pope.* 10 vols. 1886. Reprint. New York: Gordian Press, 1967.

"A new edition including several hundred letters and other new materials."

13. Heath-Stubbs, John (ed.). *Selected Poems.* New York: Barnes & Noble, 1966.

Heath-Stubbs' introduction is a biography of Pope, while his commentary is a brief discussion of the poems selected for this text.

14. Mack, Maynard (ed.). *An Essay on Man.* Twickenham Edition of the Poems of Alexander Pope, vol. III, pt. 1. London: Methuen, 1950.

Mack's comprehensive introduction provides a detailed interpretation of *Essay on Man.* Mack examines the plan, history, composition, publication, and reception of the poem; investigates Pope's philosophical and theological ideas; studies Pope's theory of the ruling passion; considers the poem on the basis of Renaissance thought and literature; and analyzes the subject, structure, and thematic pattern of the poem. See also 426 and 469.

Reviewed by Gwyn Jones, *MLR*, XLVI (1951), 488–89; Geoffrey Tillotson, *English*, VIII (1952), 203–4; Clarence Tracy, *QQ*, LVIII (1952), 448–50; Arthur Friedman, *PQ*, XXXI (1952), 290–93; Harold Williams, *RES*, n.s., III (1952), 181–83.

15. Mack, Maynard (ed.). *The Iliad of Homer, Books I-XXIV*. Twickenham Edition of the Poems of Alexander Pope, vols. VII, VIII. London: Methuen, 1967.

Mack's extensive introduction provides a detailed discussion of Pope's *Iliad* and *Odyssey* and of Pope's knowledge of Greek learning, Homer, his English predecessors, and the relationship of Pope's translation to his life and work. Also provided are the text of the *Iliad*, textual notes, and twenty-two plates.

16. ———. *The Odyssey of Homer, Books I–XXIV*. Twickenham Edition of the Poems of Alexander Pope, vols. IX, X. London: Methuen, 1967.

Provides the text of "A General View of the Epic Poem and of the *Iliad* and *Odyssey*," which is extracted from Le Bossu's *Traité du poëme épique* (Paris, 1675), the text of the *Odyssey* with textual notes, twenty-two plates, and nine appendices.

17. *Morris, E. E. (ed.). *Essay on Man; Epistles I–IV*. London: Macmillan, 1960.

18. Quennell, Peter (ed.). *The Pleasures of Pope*. New York: Pantheon Books, 1950.

Contains "a representative selection" of Pope's poetry. In his foreword, Quennell provides a general discussion of Pope's versification and wit. See also 205.

Reviewed in *TLS*, November 4, 1950, pp. 705–7; Desmond MacCarthy, *Sunday Times* (London), December 25, 1950, p. 3; Monroe K. Spears, *SR*, LX (1952), 336–47.

19. Sutherland, James R. (ed.). *The Dunciad*. Twickenham

Edition of the Poems of Alexander Pope, vol. v. 2d ed. rev. London: Methuen, 1953.

This revision of the first edition which appeared in 1943 "corrected a few mis-statements and misprints, reconsidered two passages in the Introduction, and supplied some additional annotation" (p. vi). Sutherland's lengthy introduction deals with the circumstances leading to the publication of the *Dunciad*, the history of the texts, Pope's sources, and a general interpretation of the poem. The texts are followed by a biographical appendix to the dunces which supplements Pope's own notes. See also 540 and 581.

20. Tillotson, Geoffrey (ed.). *The Rape of the Lock and Other Poems.* Twickenham Edition of the Poems of Alexander Pope, vol. II. 2d ed. rev. London: Methuen, 1954.

This revision of the 1940 edition contains ninety changes, especially pertaining to *Rape of the Lock,* some new and revised notes, and an appendix to the poem. A reset third edition with "new editorial matter" appeared in 1962. See also 398 and 403.

21. Wellington, James E. (ed.). *Epistles to Several Persons (Moral Essays).* University of Miami Critical Studies, no. 2. Coral Gables, Fla.: University of Miami Press, 1963.

Provides a comprehensive introduction to each of the four epistles, in which Wellington discusses the history of publication; studies the numerous parallels between the *Moral Essays, Imitations of Horace,* and the *Dunciad*; and analyzes the thematic relationship between the epistles and *Essay on Man.*

22. Wimsatt, William Kurtz, Jr. (ed.). *Alexander Pope: Selected Poetry and Prose.* New York: Rinehart, 1951.

Wimsatt's detailed introduction contains a chronological summary of Pope's career; a discussion of Pope's use of satire, irony, diction, and wit; and a general explication of the *Essay on Criticism, Essay on Man, Rape of the Lock,* and *Dunciad.*

BIBLIOGRAPHY

23. Griffith, Reginald Harvey. *Alexander Pope: A Bibliography. Pope's Own Writings.* London: Holland Press, 1962.

Griffith's photolith edition, which is limited to 350 copies, is divided into two volumes: volume I, 1709–1734; and volume II, 1735–1751. See also 24.

Reviewed by D. G. Neill, *BC*, XII (1963), 244, 247.

24. Hagedorn, Ralph. "Pope Bibliography," *N&Q*, CXCII (1947), 388.

Indicates that item 71 of Griffith's bibliography (see 23), which states that the fifth edition of *Essay on Criticism* appeared in 1717, must be in error, since Hagedorn has in his possession a 1716 copy, and since the collation of the fifth edition printed by Lintot in 1716 agrees with that of Lintot's fifth of 1717, but not with the edition published by T. Johnson in 1716.

25. Peavy, Charles Druery, III. "The Pope-Cibber Controversy: A Bibliography," *RECTR*, vol. III, no. 2 (1964), pp. 51–55.

Provides a briefly annotated bibliography of thirty-four items relating to the Pope-Cibber controversy.

26. Tobin, James Edward. *Alexander Pope: A List of Critical Studies Published from 1895 to 1944.* New York: Cosmopolitan Science & Art Service, 1945.

Tobin's list is supplemented by this bibliography. Tobin's annotations are "kept to a minimum" (p. 3).

Reviewed by J. C. Mendenhall, *Thought*, XX (1945), 553–54; John Butt, *RES*, XXIII (1947), 177–79.

MANUSCRIPTS

27. Butt, John. "Pope's Poetical Manuscripts." Warton Lecture on English Poetry, 1954. *PBA*, XL (1954), 23–39.

Provides a study of Pope's manuscripts, an appendix which lists the present location of fifty-five autograph manuscripts, and six plates which are reproductions of the Morgan manuscript of *Epistle to Dr. Arbuthnot.* See also 219.

Reviewed by David Ramage, *DUJ*, XLVIII (1956), 125–26; Norman Callan, *RES*, n.s., IX (1958), 119.

28. ———. "A Prose Fragment Wrongly Attributed to Gay and Pope," *N&Q*, CC (1955), 23–25.

Argues that A. L. McLeod's transcription of the manuscript in the Pierpont Morgan Library (see 35) is "not altogether accurate" and that Pope was not the author of the fragment relating to a dream, but that Fortesque was probably the author of the "vision" fragment rather than Pope.

29. Dearing, Vinton A. "The Prince of Wales's Set of Pope's Works," *HLB*, IV (1950), 320–38.

Provides a detailed description of revisions made in a four-volume set of Pope's *Works* (1717); *Works*, volume II, 1735; and *Letters* (1737). Dearing also examines the bibliographical and biographical significance of the set. See also 219.

30. Foxon, David F. "Concealed Pope Editions," *BC*, V (1956), 277–79.

Confirms William B. Todd's conclusions (see 40) about the *First and Second Epistles of the Second Book of Horace.*

31. ———. "Two Cruces in Pope Bibliography," *TLS*, January 24, 1958, p. 52.

Foxon states that the large folio on *Essay on Man* is the first issue of the poem, but that the "octavo as a whole has no priority, even of impression, over the duodecimo" for the first edition of the *Dunciad.*

32. Guerinot, Joseph V. (ed.). *Two Poems against Pope: One Epistle to Mr. A. Pope, Leonard Welsted (1730); The Blatant Beast, Anonymous (1740)*. Augustan Reprint Society, no. 114. Los Angeles: Clark Memorial Library, University of California, 1965.

> Reprints and comments on both attacks. Guerinot states that both pamphlets are examples "of the calumny, detraction, and critical misunderstanding Pope endured . . ." (p. i).

33. Mack, Maynard. "A Manuscript of Pope's *Imitation of the First Ode of the Fourth Book of Horace*," *MLN*, LX (1945), 185–88.

> Provides a transcription of Pope's manuscript in "Spence's hand." Mack finds that the "manuscript version . . ." is "different in text and orthography from the published poem" (p. 185) and suggests that "Spence's copy was taken from some late state of the poem . . ." (p. 188) before it was further revised and published.

34. ———. "Two Variant Copies of Pope's *Works . . . Volume II*: Further Light on Some Problems of Authorship, Bibliography, and Text," *The Library*, 5th ser., XII (1957), 48–53.

> Examines two variant copies of Pope's *Works*. Mack concludes that the two volumes indicate the following: "Pope originally intended to collect *The Dunciad* into one volume with the Scriblerus prose" (p. 48); both Pope and Gay are the authors of *Guardian*, no. 2; and at one time, Pope had planned to cancel from his canon *Guardian*, no. 2, and *Guardian*, no. 40.

35. McLeod, A. L. "Pope and Gay: Two Overlooked Manuscripts," *N&Q*, CXCVIII (1953), 334–37.

> Discusses two documents in the Pierpont Morgan Library's collection of autograph manuscripts: a letter to William Fortesque and "a prose composition relating a dream" (p. 34). McLeod finds that the letter is "an authentic Gay manuscript" (p. 34), but that the prose composition is a Pope manuscript. McLeod includes a copy of the letter and the dream composition. See also 28.

36. *Pope, Alexander. *An Essay on Man. Reproduction of the Manuscripts in the Pierpont Morgan Library and the Houghton Library, with the Printed Text of the Original Edition.* Introduction by Maynard Mack. Oxford: Oxford University Press for the Roxburghe Club, 1962.

37. Schmitz, Robert M. "Two New Holographs of Pope's Birthday Lines to Martha Blount," *RES*, n.s., VIII (1957), 234–40.

> Provides the text of the holograph (located in the Pierpont Morgan Library) which directly challenges the primacy of Norman Ault's "original" of the "a" text of the poem (see 165). Schmitz describes the manuscript, compares it with other versions of the text, and explains Pope's use of the text for Martha as well as for a "poetical flirtation" with Judith Cowper.

38. Sherburn, George. "The Swift-Pope *Miscellanies* of 1732," *HLB*, VI (1952), 387–90.

> Prints and examines the significance of "a hitherto unknown document in the hand of Jonathan Swift [which] helps to clarify the confused proceedings that accompanied the publication . . . of the final volume of the *Miscellanies*." Sherburn states that Pope was not trying to make more money for himself by having publishers compete with each other. See also 39.

39. ———. "The Swift-Pope *Miscellanies* of 1732: Corrigendum," *HLB*, VII (1953), 248.

> Corrects his statement (see 38) that the document was "hitherto unknown." Sherburn states that the document was previously printed by John Nichols in 1779 and in the appendix to Scott's edition of Swift's *Works* (1814).

40. Todd, William B. "Concealed Pope Editions," *BC*, V (1956), 48–52.

> Distinguishes the variant editions of the *Epistle to Burlington, Epistle to Bathurst,* and *First and Second Epistles of the Second Book of Horace,* "as variously represented by seventy-three copies in twelve libraries" (p. 48). Todd concludes that "for many of the editions now on record there are as many more hidden under the same general description . . ." (p. 48). See also 30.

BIOGRAPHY

41. Ault, Norman. "Pope and Addison," *Essential Articles for the Study of Alexander Pope.* Edited by Maynard Mack. Hamden, Conn.: Shoestring Press, 1964.

> Provides a detailed account of the biographical events surrounding Pope's acquaintance with and subsequent attack on Addison. Ault repudiates "the charge of treachery against Pope, and establishes both the early date and Addison's knowledge of the satire" (p. 476) before his death. See also 165 and 219.

42. Benét, William Rose. "Alexander Pope," *SRL*, xxix (April 13, 1946), 94–95.

> Provides a reproduction of a self-portrait of Pope, briefly comments on Pope's training under Charles Jervas, and states that the background of Pope's portrait "is identical with an original sepia sketch which serves as the frontispiece of Warburton's edition of *An Essay on Man*" (p. 95).

43. Booth, Edward Townsend. *God Made the Country.* New York: Alfred A. Knopf, 1946.

> Contains brief biographical comments on Pope's life and works.

44. Boyce, Benjamin. "Mr. Pope, in Bath, Improves the Design of His Grotto," *Restoration and Eighteenth-Century Literature. Essays in Honor of Alan Dugald McKillop.* Edited by Carroll Camden. Chicago: University of Chicago Press for William Marsh Rice University, 1963.

> Describes changes and additions made by Pope in his grotto, emphasizes Pope's debt to Rev. William Borlase and Dr. William Oliver, and states that the effect Pope wanted in his grotto was "a faithful representation of nature." Boyce also provides an "ink sketch drawn by Pope" of the poet's grotto. See also 182.

45. ———. "The Poet and the Postmaster: The Friendship of Alexander Pope and Ralph Allen," *PQ,* xlv (January, 1966), 114–22.

Describes Pope's acquaintance and subsequent friendship with Ralph Allen, compares Pope's ideas and writings with Allen's activities and interest in Pope's correspondence, and discusses Pope's influence on Allen's mansion and grounds at Prior Park.

46. Bracher, Frederick. "Pope's Grotto: The Maze of Fancy," *HLQ*, XII (1949), 114–62.

Recount's the tradition of the garden-grotto, compares it with Pope's grotto, provides a detailed description of Pope's grotto and its twenty-year development, and examines Pope's taste and personality as reflected by his grotto. Bracher concludes that Pope turned "the grotto into a combination of *nymphaeum*, rococo fairyland, and museum for virtuosi" (p. 162). See also 219.

47. Brownell, Morris Ruggles. "Alexander Pope, Virtuoso." Unpublished Ph.D. dissertation, University of California, Berkeley, 1966, *DA*, XXVII (1967), 3421–22.

Examines Pope's "virtuosoship" in the humanist tradition; provides an account of Pope's taste in the fine arts by studying "precept, practice, poetic sensibility, and contemporary influence"; and discusses Pope's taste in landscape gardening, painting, architecture, sculpture, and music.

48. Burgess, C. F. "The Footman and Mr. Pope's Trial by Water," *Cithara*, III (1963), 80–81.

States that the footman who rescued Pope from drowning has received undeserved neglect.

49. Dobrée, Bonamy. *Alexander Pope*. London: Sylvan Press, 1951.

Dobrée provides a comprehensive biographical discussion of Pope and a general critical study of his works.

Reviewed by Norman Knox, *SAQ*, LI (1952), 467; Rebecca Price Parkin, *WHR*, VI (1952), 300–301; *TLS*, December 14, 1951, p. 806; E. Audra, *EA*, VI (1953), 260–61; Irène Simon, *ES*, XXXV (1953), 85–88.

50. Dyson, H. V. D., and Butt, John. *Augustans and Romantics*. 2d ed. Introductions to English Literature, edited by Bon-

amy Dobrée, vol. III. New York: Dover Publications, 1954.

Contains a brief biographical and interpretative sketch and a selective annotated bibliography of contemporary editions of Pope's works and modern criticism to 1945.

51. Halsband, Robert. "Pope, Lady Mary, and the *Court Poems* (1716)," *PMLA*, LXVIII (1953), 237–50.

Cites "valuable new data" (p. 237) in order to determine the authorship of the *Court Poems* and the motivation for Pope's "emetic" revenge on Curll. Halsband concludes that Pope primarily was motivated to protect John Gay, not Lady Mary.

52. ———. "Two New Letters from Lady Mary Wortley Montagu to Alexander Pope," *PQ*, XXIX (1950), 349–52.

Ascribes two letters found "among Pope's Homer MSS" (p. 349) to Lady Mary. Halsband suggests that the letters reveal that Pope's friendship with Lady Mary "lasted longer than has previously been thought" (p. 352).

53. Henderson, Anthony Gordon. "Pope and the Poet's Environment." Unpublished Ph.D. dissertation, Columbia University, 1967, *DA*, XXVIII (1967), 631–32.

In exploring "the interaction between man and his milieu" and Pope's "defense of himself as an artist and a good man," produced by Pope's "references in his poetry and correspondence to the places where he lived and where other men choose to live," Henderson examines "eighteenth-century geology, economic theory, gardening manuals, land-scape design," and the "philosophic background" for Pope's love "of life in the country."

54. Highet, Gilbert. *The Powers of Poetry*. New York: Oxford University Press, 1960.

In his chapter entitled "Pope: The Lady and the Poet," Highet describes Pope's "malignant caricature" of Lady Mary Wortley Montagu and states that Pope's "vile couplet" (*Dunciad*, II, 135–36) was the start of his public attack on Lady Mary.

55. Jacobs, Elijah L. "The Amiable Lady Mary," *SAQ*, LVIII (1959), 381–92.

Provides an account of Pope's friendship and subsequent quarrel with Lady Mary Wortley Montagu. Jacobs emphasizes Lady Mary's vitriolic wit, a quality which enabled her to "match wits" with Pope.

56. Kronenberger, Louis. "Pope—Demi-Devil or Child of Pain?" *SRL*, xxx (December 13, 1947), 9–10, 29–30.

Contains a brief biographical account of Pope.

57. ———. *The Republic of Letters: Essays on Various Writers*. New York: Alfred A. Knopf, 1955.

In chapter three, Kronenberger provides an account of Pope's life; discusses Pope's most "biased" biographers, Elwin and Sitwell; describes Pope's intrigues in publishing his correspondence; and comments on Pope as a moral poet.

58. Lewis, David Earle. "A Quarrelsome Romance of the Eighteenth Century," *DR*, xxvi (1946), 198–202.

Discusses Pope's relationship with Lady Mary Wortley Montagu.

59. Lynch, Harry. "Pope's Willow," *AN&Q*, iv (1945), 188.

States that a reference to Pope as the father of "the willow-trees along the Housatonic" refers to Samuel Johnson (of Stratford, Connecticut), who received from Pope cuttings from the Twickenham willow, which he planted in Connecticut.

60. MacDonald, Wilbert Lorne. "A French Life of Pope," *UTQ*, xv (1946), 193–95.

Comments on the inaccurate and misleading information supplied by Ruffhead and other early Popean biographers. MacDonald cites and describes a French critical biography of Pope, *Oeuvres diverses de Pope, traduites de l'anglois*, printed in 1753, as more instructive and "admirable" than contemporary English attempts.

61. Mack, Maynard. "A Poet in His Landscape: Pope at Twickenham," *From Sensibility to Romanticism: Essays Presented to Frederick A. Pottle*. Edited by Frederick W.

Hilles and Harold Bloom. New York: Oxford University Press, 1965.

Focusing on the "historical and biographical" aspects of Pope's estate, Mack "reconstructs . . . a reliable account of the poet's house and garden as they were . . . between 1719 and 1744—without, however, abandoning the effort to understand what they may have contributed to the life of his poetic imagination" (p. 3). See also 209.

62. Mahaffey, Lois Kathleen. "Alexander Pope and His Sappho: Pope's Relationship with Lady Mary Wortley Montagu and Its Influence on His Work." Unpublished Ph.D. dissertation, University of Texas, 1963, *DA*, XXIV (1963), 2480.

In examining the biographical problem related to Pope's friendship, then estrangement, with Lady Mary, Mahaffey "attempts to correct the chronology of . . . thirty-three of Pope's letters" and to reconstruct Montagu's letters to Pope. Mahaffey concludes that Pope's "one *grande passion* was for Lady Mary" and that the subsequent "estrangement was the result of a Lesbian attachment between Lady Mary and Maria Skerrett."

63. Malins, Edward. *English Landscaping and Literature, 1660-1840*. London: Oxford University Press, 1966.

Chapter two, "Kent, Burlington, Pope and Friends," contains references to Pope's garden at Twickenham.

64. Moore, John Robert. "Pope's Grotto and Wookey Hole," *N&Q*, CCX (1965), 217–18.

Suggests the possibility that Pope may have illegally ordered the removal of the stalactites from Wookey Hole in order that they be placed in his grotto.

65. Osborn, James M. "Spence, Natural Genius and Pope," *PQ*, XLV (January, 1966), 123–44.

Describes in detail Spence's predilection for "studying untutored" prodigies and interest in helping natural geniuses to gain recognition. Spence's friendship with Pope is given as an example of Spence's interest in natural genius.

66. "Pope's Tree," *Emerson Society Quarterly,* XIII (1958), 4.

Provides an illustration of a tree near Binfield, where Pope "is said to have composed many of his earlier pieces," and reprints an article from *The Penny Magazine* (February 21, 1835) which refers to the tree.

67. Powell, Dilys. "Alexander Pope," *English Wits.* Edited by Leonard Russell. London: Hutchinson, 1953.

Contains a general biographical and interpretative sketch, with emphasis on Pope's wit and satire.

68. Rippy, Frances Mayhew. "Matthew Prior and Alexander Pope: Their Personal and Literary Relationship." Unpublished Ph.D. dissertation, Vanderbilt University, 1957, *DA,* XVII (1957), 1754–55.

Substantiates Prior's and Pope's informal but not intimate relationship; discusses Pope's high regard for Prior's artistry and Pope's role in compiling and editing Prior's works; and examines Pope's debt to Prior in *Eloisa to Abelard, Essay on Man, Imitation of the Sixth Satire of the Second Book of Horace,* and *First Ode of the Fourth Book of Horace.*

69. Ryley, Robert Michael. "Warburton, Warton, and Ruffhead's *Life of Pope,*" *PLL,* IV (Winter, 1968), 51–62.

Provides an analysis of Ruffhead's and Warburton's roles in writing the *Life of Pope.* Ryley concludes that "every passage of criticism that can be defined as his (Ruffhead's) is either dead wrong or highly dubious" and that Warburton did try to "minimize" Ruffhead's errors by Warburton's objections and revisions of the proof sheets.

70. Sherburn, George. "An Accident in 1726," *HLB,* II (1948), 121–23.

Provides a biographical account of an accident (which nearly caused Pope to drown), the man who saved the poet, Pope's recovery, and Pope's expression of gratitude.

71. ———. "Pope on the Threshold of His Career," *HLB,* XIII (1959), 29–46.

Describes Pope's early education, activities, and friends.

Sherburn focuses on William Trumbull's influence on Pope's reading and considers the literary significance of Pope's relationship with Trumbull.

72. Spence, Joseph. *Observations, Anecdotes, and Characters of Books and Men, Collected from Conversation.* Edited by James M. Osborn. Oxford: Clarendon Press, 1966.

Part I contains anecdotes by and about Pope; part II contains nine appendices related to Pope, plus Spence's entry under "Pope" in the index to the Huntington manuscript of the anecdotes.

73. Wimsatt, William Kurtz, Jr. "An Image of Pope," *From Sensibility to Romanticism: Essays Presented to Frederick A. Pottle.* Edited by Frederick W. Hilles and Harold Bloom. New York: Oxford University Press, 1965.

Reproduces and examines six pictures of Pope. Wimsatt discusses the historical aspects of the pictures and attempts to reveal their relationship with one another. See also 209.

74. ———. *The Portraits of Alexander Pope.* New Haven: Yale University Press, 1965.

Provides an extensive "guide to the portraiture of Pope" and a biography of Pope. The approximately 205 pictures of Pope are "arranged in a nearly biographical or chronological order" (p. xxxii).

Reviewed by Robert M. Schmitz, *PQ*, XLV (1966), 580-81.

POPE AS A CRITIC

75. Atkins, J. W. H. *English Literary Criticism: 17th and 18th Centuries.* London: Methuen, 1951.

> Contains various sections that focus on Pope's critical theory and judgment as observed in his *Essay on Criticism*, Preface of Editor to *Shakespeare, Art of Sinking in Poetry*, and *Epistle to Augustus*. Atkins briefly mentions the following Popean critics: Dennis, Wharton, Johnson, and Cowper.

76. Dearing, Vinton A. "Pope, Theobald, and Wycherley's *Posthumous Works,*" *PMLA,* LXVIII (1953), 223–36.

> Examines Pope's edition of the *Posthumous Works of William Wycherley* and compares it with Theobald's edition. Dearing considers the authorship of various sections of Pope's edition, questions the authenticity of several poems usually ascribed to Wycherley, and comments on Pope's revisions of Wycherley's poems.

77. Elledge, Scott (ed.). *Eighteenth-Century Critical Essays,* vol. I. Ithaca: Cornell University Press, 1961.

> Reprints "Pope's chief essays in explicit criticism" (p. 530): *Guardian*, no. 40; Preface to *Iliad* (1715); Preface of Editor to *Shakespeare*; and Postscript to *Odyssey*. Elledge provides general background information and interpretation of the four texts, plus sixty-five explanatory notes to the texts, and reprints Joseph Spence's "Essay on Pope's *Odyssey*" and the text from Joseph Warton's *Essay on the Genius and Writings of Pope*.

78. Ellis, William D., Jr. "Thomas D'Urfey, the Pope-Philips Quarrel, and *The Shepherd's Week,*" *PMLA,* LXXIV (1959), 203–12.

> Maintains that the rustic songs and ballads of Thomas D'Urfey influenced the Pope-Philips quarrel and Gay's *Shepherd's Week*. Ellis states that Pope equated D'Urfey's ballads with Philips' pastorals in order to criticize Philips.

79. Goldgar, Bertrand A. (ed.). *Literary Criticism of Alex-*

ander Pope. Regents Critics Series. Lincoln: University of
Nebraska Press, 1965.

Placing Pope's literary criticism under the following
headings: pastoral poetry, epic poetry, drama, and general
theory, Goldgar provides the texts of the *Essay on Criticism*; Preface to *Works* (1717); selections from Pope's
correspondence; *Peri Bathous*; *Discourse on Pastoral
Poetry*; *Guardian*, no. 40; Preface to *Iliad*; Pope's observations on the *Iliad*; Postscript to *Odyssey*; and the Preface to
Shakespeare. In his extensive introduction, Goldgar analyzes the history of Pope's criticism, studies Pope's methods
as a critic, and interprets Pope's critical principles.

80. Goldstein, Malcolm. *Pope and the Augustan Stage.* Stanford Studies in Language and Literature, no. 17. Stanford:
Stanford University Press, 1958.

Examines Pope's theatrical relationships, interest, and
participation in such works as *Three Hours after Marriage*;
describes Pope's activity as a consultant in reading new
manuscripts, in rendering advice or an opinion, and in re-
vising or writing prologues or epilogues; and studies Pope's
role as a critic of actors, managers, playwrights, and theatrical productions.

Reviewed by Arthur H. Scouten, *PQ*, XXXVIII (1959), 341;
Willard H. Bonner, *MLJ*, XLIII (1959), 54–55; Oliver
W. Ferguson, *SAQ*, LVIII (1959), 622–23; Jacques Golliet,
EA, XII (1959), 249; Robert W. Rogers, *JEGP*, LVIII (1959),
301–2; *TLS*, January 16, 1959, p. 30; Aubrey L. Williams,
MLN, LXXV (1960), 269–70.

81. Griffith, Reginald Harvey. "Pope on the Art of Gardening," *Texas University Department of English, Studies in
English*, XXXI (1952), 52–56.

States that Pope's task of correcting the third edition
of James Gardiner's translation of René Rapin's gardening
poem *Hortorum Libri* should be included in Pope's bibliography. Griffith describes Pope's relationship with Walter
Harte, an eighteen-year-old collaborator in correcting the
edition, and concludes that Pope's editorial attitude (as compared with Harte) "was conservative and commonsensible"
(p. 54).

82. Huseboe, Arthur Robert. "Pope's Critical Views of the

London Stage," *RECTR*, vol. III, no. 1 (1964), pp. 25–37.

Studies Pope's "comprehensive criticism of the drama contained in the *Dunciad, To Augustus,* but especially in *Peri Bathous.*" Huseboe divides Pope's attacks on Augustan opera and theatre as: (1) Pope "examines the language and genre of the plays and finds them indecorous; (2) he is critical of sensational appeal; and (3) he satirizes the character of those associated with the theatre" (p. 28).

83. Hynes, Samuel L. (ed). *English Literary Criticism: Restoration and 18th Century.* New York: Appleton-Century-Crofts, 1963.

Provides the texts of Pope's *Essay on Criticism* and *Discourse on Pastoral Poetry.*

84. Nixon, Howard Kenneth, Jr. "The Literary Theories of Alexander Pope." Unpublished Ph.D. dissertation, University of Illinois, 1961, *DA,* XXII (1961), 1614–15.

Collects Pope's critical comments from his poetry, prose, correspondence, editions, and his conversations with Joseph Spence and maintains that these comments are derived from "consistent and unified aesthetic principles" (p. 1614) and that Pope's literary theories, based on nature, provide the poet with "a basis for his artistic doctrines" (p. 1615).

85. Perella, Nicholas J. "Amarilli's Dilemma: the *Pastor Fido* and Some English Authors," *CL,* XII (1960), 348-59.

States that Giambattista Guarini's pastoral tragicomedy *Pastor Fido* was for Pope "a focal point in determining what pastoral poetry should not be like" (p. 351).

86. ———. "Pope's Judgment of the *Pastor Fido* and a Case of Plagiarism," *PQ,* XL (1961), 444–48.

Cites Pope's July 2, 1706, letter to Walsh in which he adversely criticized Guarini's *Pastor Fido* "because it failed to be simple and rustic" (p. 447), and reprints an excerpt from the announcement to the 1736 edition of Richard Fanshawe's translation of Guarini's play, which not only plagiarized Pope's letter, but turned the criticism into praise for the work.

87. Reichard, Hugo M. "The Independence of Pope as a Political Satirist," *JEGP,* LIV (1955), 309–17.

> Examines the range and intensity of Pope's political and social satire, which "rigorously exposes the evils of a money culture in all strata and quarters" (p. 314). Reichard concludes that, "while Pope is indebted to the (Patriot) Opposition for many of his satiric concepts, he goes beyond the party organs in the scope of his criticism of the Quality; and he goes counter to party tactics in leveling criticism at the business community as a whole" (p. 317).

88. Rogal, Samuel J. "Pope's Treatment of Colley Cibber," *Lock Haven Review,* no. 8 (1966), pp. 25–30.

> Concludes that Pope instigated and maintained his feud with Cibber because of Pope's dislike for the "eighteenth-century comic stage, his utter disrespect for the position of poet laureate, and his almost sadistic delight in attacking persons who were either inept at or indifferent to mounting a concentrated counter-attack" (p. 25).

89. Ruhe, E. L. "Pope's Hand in Thomas Birch's Account of Gay," *RES,* n.s., V (1954), 171–74.

> Prints "a hitherto unpublished and unknown letter of Pope's copied out in Birch's hand" (p. 171) which relates to Birch's biography of John Gay. The letter contains Pope's refusal to have his name used in conjunction with the biography; however, Pope made suggestions for revision which were followed. Ruhe also cites evidence that Pope did "gloss over" the proof sheets of the biography.

90. Sullivan, J. P. (ed.). "Alexander Pope on Classics and Classicists," *Arion,* V (1966), 235–53.

> Provides a brief critical introduction to a representative selection of Pope's "critical remarks on ancient authors."

91. Thorpe, James (ed.). *Milton Criticism.* New York: Rinehart, 1950.

> Provides an excerpt from Pope's Postscript to *Odyssey* (1723) which contains a brief commentary on Milton and his imitators.

POPE AS A SOURCE OR INFLUENCE

92. Aden, John M. "Pope's Horace in Johnson's Juvenal," *N&Q*, CCVI (1961), 254–55.

Suggests that Johnson's *Vanity of Human Wishes*, II, 305–6, was influenced by Pope's translation of Horace's *Second Epistle of the Second Book*, II, 72–73.

93. *Battestin, Martin C. "Pope's *Magus* in Fielding's Veroniad: The Satire of Walpole," *PQ*, XLVI (1967), 137–41.

94. Beaty, Frederick L. " 'Ae Spark o' Nature's Fire,' " *ELN*, I (1964), 203–7.

Demonstrates that stanza 13 from Burns' "Epistle to J. Lapraik, an Old Scottish Bard, April 1, 1785," owes a debt not only to a passage in Sterne's *Tristram Shandy*, but also to lines 195–96 of part I of Pope's *Essay on Criticism*.

95. Beck, Richard. "Alexander Pope and Icelandic Literature," *Scandinavian Studies*, XXV (1953), 37–45.

Examines eighteenth-century Icelandic translations of Pope's *Universal Prayer, Essay on Man*, and *Essay on Criticism*, and the extent to which those poems influenced Icelandic poets.

96. Burgess, C. F. "The Genesis of *The Beggar's Opera*," *Cithara*, II (1962), 6–12.

States that Gay's debt to Pope, Swift, and Arbuthnot constitutes "casual assistance" and not literary dependence. Burgess concludes that Gay's indebtedness to Swift for *The Beggar's Opera* "has been seriously exaggerated" (p. 6).

97. Dale, James. "Pope's 'Wayward Queen' and a Letter from Gray," *N&Q*, CCVII (1962), 459.

Points out that a sentence from Gray's letter to West contains an allusion to *Rape of the Lock*, IV, 57–58.

98. Effross, Susi H. "The Influence of Alexander Pope in Eighteenth-Century Spain," *SP*, LXIII (1966), 78–92.

Finds "(1) that [E. Allison] Peers's assessment of Pope's Spanish fortunes is inaccurate; (2) that Pope's influence hinged not only on his 'neo-classical' and Philosophical poems, but extended also to the plaintive *Eloisa to Abelard* . . . ; and (3) that Spanish interest in Pope was to a large extent the direct result of the English poet's great popularity in France" (p. 78).

99. Fabian, Bernhard. "German Echoes of a Famous Popean Line," *N&Q*, CCIII (1958), 18–20.

Suggests the extent to which *Essay on Man*, II, 1–2, has "pervaded contemporary thought" since Lessing, Goethe, and Moritz inserted the opening couplet "almost verbatim in their own works" (p. 18).

100. Forcione, Alban. "Meléndez Valdés and the *Essay on Man*," *Hispanic Review*, XXXIV (1966), 291–306.

Substantiates the "extraordinary popularity of Pope" in eighteenth-century France and Spain and asserts that Meléndez Valdés' 1797 edition of his poetry "was directly inspired . . . in ideas, construction, and phrases . . . by Pope's *Essay on Man*" (p. 293).

101. Greany, Helen T. "Some Interesting Parallels: Pope and the Paycock," *N&Q*, CCIII (1958), 253.

Finds that O'Casey in the final act of *Juno and the Paycock* borrowed from line 248 of *Essay on Man*, IV.

102. Hart, Jeffery P. "T. S. Eliot: His Use of Wycherley and Pope," *N&Q*, CCII (1957), 389–90.

Suggests that Pope's *Dunciad*, III, is echoed by Eliot in *Gerontion*.

103. Hutchens, Eleanor N. "Gray's Cat and Pope's Belinda," *TSL*, VI (1961), 103–8.

Finding close parallels between Selima's misfortunes and Belinda's treatment, Hutchens states that Gray's "Ode on the Death of a Favourite Cat" was based on the plot, characterization, and setting of *Rape of the Lock*.

104. Kishler, Thomas C. "The Sacred Rites of Pride: An Echo of *The Rape of the Lock* in *Babbitt*," *SNL*, III (1965), 28–29.

Notes a "parallel in Lewis' *Babbitt* (chapter five, section III) which reflects in spirit, if not in every detail . . ." *Rape of the Lock*, I, 121–28.

105. Korte, Donald M. "Tobias Smollett's *Advice* and *Reproof*," *Thoth*, vol. VII, no. 2 (Spring, 1967), pp. 45–65.

Indicates that "Smollett's two formal verse satires . . . are both two speaker dialogues modelled in structure, theme, and wording after various Pope satires."

106. Leach, Frederick D. "Hogarth's *Distressed Poet*: The Riddle of the Garret," *Ohio University Review*, II (1960), 5–20.

Provides a reproduction of William Hogarth's painting and the two prints made from it. Leach explains that the painting *Distressed Poet* probably was initially inspired by the *Dunciad* and that the two prints contain allusions to Pope.

107. Lee, Jae Ho. "Alexander Pope in Eliot's 'East Coker,' " *N&Q*, CCVIII (1963), 381.

Notes a parallel between Eliot's "Four Quartets," section IV of "East Coker," and lines 143–46 of Pope's *Essay on Man*.

108. Litz, Francis E. "Pope and Twickenham's Famous Preacher," *MLQ*, XVII (1956), 204–12.

Cites numerous passages from the sermons of Jeremiah Seed, curate of Twickenham Chapel from 1733 to 1742, and examines Seed's indebtedness to Pope's *Essay on Criticism* and *Essay on Man*, which "seem to have influenced him deeply" (p. 205).

109. Lombard, C. M. "Pope and Lamartine," *N&Q*, CXCIX (1954), 287–88.

States that Pope's *Universal Prayer* had an indirect influence on Lamartine's "La Prière" (a poem in the *Premières Méditations*).

110. MacLaine, Allan H. "Shelley's *The Cloud* and Pope's *Rape*

of the Lock: An Unsuspected Link," *Keats-Shelley Journal*, VIII (1959), 14–16.

Demonstrates that Shelley "was indebted" to canto II of *Rape of the Lock* "not only for several details and phrases, but also for the general artistic method" (p. 14) of *The Cloud*.

111. Maxwell, J. C. "Gray's Cat as Helen of Troy," *N&Q*, CXCIX (1954), 314.

Cites two lines of Gray's "Ode on the Death of a Favourite Cat" as a "heroic echo" of Pope's *Iliad*, III, 473–74.

112. ————. "Hume: A Reference to Pope," *N&Q*, CCIV (1959), 404.

Indicates that a passage in David Hume's earliest surviving letter is an allusion to Pope's *Essay on Criticism*, III, 679–80. See also 357.

113. ————. "Melville Allusion to Pope," *AN&Q*, III (1964), 7.

Reveals the close parallel between Melville's *Redburn* (chapter thirty) and Pope's *Epistle to Arbuthnot*, I, 4.

114. ————. " 'Talk Dead': Pope and Johnson," *N&Q*, CCVIII (1963), 220.

Indicates that Johnson's *London*, line 18, is indebted to line 624 of Pope's *Essay on Criticism*.

115. Newton, Frances J. "Venice, Pope, T. S. Eliot and D. H. Lawrence," *N&Q*, CCIII (1958), 119–20.

Reveals parallel passages in Pope's *Essay on Man*, Eliot's *Gerontion*, and Lawrence's *Lady Chatterley's Lover* to substantiate his contention that all three employed Venice as "a valid symbol to illustrate and comment on the evolution of [their] society" (p. 120).

116. Price, Frances. "Alice Meynell and the *Essay on Man*," *N&Q*, CXCII (1947), 430.

Claims that two of Meynell's poems, "Christ in the Universe" and "To the Body," reflect lines 21–28 and 131–40 of *Essay on Man*, I.

117. Reaves, R. B., Jr. "Borrowings from Pope in Thomson," *N&Q*, CCVII (1962), 459.

Finds that Thomson directly borrowed from Pope's *Windsor Forest* in a passage from *The Castle of Indolence* as well as in "Lines on Marlefield."

118. Roberts, Mark. "A Note on Gray's 'Elegy,'" *ES*, XXXIX (1958), 251–56.

Finds close parallels between the imagery of Gray's "Elegy" and Pope's *Rape of the Lock* and *Epistle to Dr. Arbuthnot*. Roberts suggests that Gray was very conscious of Pope's lines and hoped his readers would realize his debt to Pope.

119. Shaver, Chester L. "A Wordsworth-Pope Parallel," *MLN*, LXI (1946), 467–68.

Suggests that Wordsworth's famous line ("If thou indeed derive thy light from Heaven") echoes lines 11–13 of *Essay on Criticism*.

120. Simon, Irène. "Echoes in *The Waste Land*," *ES*, XXXIV (1953), 64–72.

Cites close parallels between Eliot's woman ("A Game of Chess") in *The Waste Land* and Pope's description of Belinda's toilet in *Rape of the Lock*.

121. Speaight, George. "Pope in the Toy Theatre," *Theatre Notebook*, VII (1953), 62–63.

Quotes lines from Greene's edition of a Victorian toy theatre play, *The Silver Palace*, which "are lifted, with slight verbal modifications, from Pope's translation of the *Iliad*" (p. 63).

122. Weatherly, Edward H. "Churchill's Literary Indebtedness to Pope," *SP*, XLIII (1946), 59–69.

Provides a detailed study of Pope's (rather than Dryden's) extensive influence on the poetry of Charles Churchill.

123. Wilson, Edmund. *The Shores of Light: A Literary Chronicle of the Twenties and Thirties.* New York: Farrar, Straus & Young, 1952.

Contains a brief chapter entitled "Pope and Tennyson" which compares the two poets and suggests Pope's influence on Tennyson.

EIGHTEENTH- AND NINETEENTH-CENTURY
CRITICISM OF POPE

124. Agate, James (comp.). *The English Dramatic Critics: An Anthology, 1660-1932.* New York: Hill & Wang, 1958.

> Contains a reprint of Leigh Hunt's criticism of Pope entitled "On Mr. Pope—'A Robustious Fellow, who tears a Passion to Tatters.'"

125. Allison, James. "Joseph Warton's Reply to Dr. Johnson's *Lives,*" *JEGP*, LI (1952), 186–91.

> Briefly studies Warton's criticism of Pope and concludes that volume II of Warton's *Essay on the Genius and Writings of Pope* was published as an intentional reply and contrast to Johnson's *Lives of the Poets.*

126. Amarasinghe, Upali. *Dryden and Pope in the Early Nineteenth Century. A Study of Changing Literary Taste, 1800-1830.* Cambridge: At the University Press, 1962.

> Contains a detailed study of the varied critical attitudes (between 1800 and 1830) of Augustan poetry, focusing on the literary reputations of Dryden and Pope; discusses the impact and the critical standards of Joseph Warton's, W. L. Bowles', and William Roscoe's editions of Pope's works; examines the critical attitudes of the *Edinburgh Review, Quarterly Review,* and *Blackwood's Edinburgh Magazine* toward the Augustans and the Romantics; includes chapters on the "Pope Controversy" (appended with a bibliography of that controversy); and concludes that the influence of the Augustans survived in the criticism and poetry of the early nineteenth century.

> Reviewed by Allan R. Bevan, *DR,* XLIII (1963), 423; John Butt, *DUJ,* n.s., XXIV (1963), 154–55; John Gross, *New Statesman,* LXV (1963), 521–22; G. D. Klingopulos, *MLR,* LVIII (1963), 245–46; *TLS,* February 1, 1962, p. 78.

127. Ames, Alfred C. "Early Criticism of Pope's 'Night-Piece,'" *MLN,* LX (1945), 265–67.

> Disagrees with Geoffrey Tillotson (*Essay in Criticism and Research* [1942]). Ames asserts that Coleridge was not

without precedent in his adverse criticism of the "night-piece" passage from book VIII of Pope's *Iliad*. Ames cites Samuel Say (1745), an anonymous critic in *London Magazine* (1782), and three other "hostile" critics of the passage.

128. Blanshard, Rufus A. (ed.). *Discussions of Alexander Pope*. Boston: Heath, 1960.

Contains the following essays: Joseph Warton's "An Essay on the Genius and Writings of Pope"; Samuel Johnson's "Alexander Pope"; William Cowper's "From Table Talk"; William Wordsworth's "Remarks on Pope"; Samuel Taylor Coleridge's "Remarks on Pope"; Lord Byron's "Some Observations upon an Article in *Blackwood's Magazine*"; William Hazlitt's "On Dryden and Pope"; John Conington's "Correctness, Homer, and Horace"; and Matthew Arnold's "Pope's Translation of Homer" and "Dryden and Pope: Classics of Our Prose."

129. Boyce, Benjamin. "Samuel Johnson's Criticism of Pope in the *Life of Pope*," *RES*, n.s., V (1954), 37–46.

Analyzes Johnson's *Life of Pope*, focusing on his indebtedness to Joseph Warton's *Essay on the Writings and Genius of Pope* and to other critics such as Robert Shiels, Warburton, and Dennis. Boyce concludes that not all of Johnson's *Life* contains valid literary criticism and that "Johnson did not initiate so much as he attempted to adjudicate; he was often writing a critique of the critics" (p. 46).

130. Carroll, John. "Richardson on Pope and Swift," *UTQ*, XXXIII (1963), 19–29.

Prints an extract from a letter to Dr. Cheyne from Samuel Richardson which contains Richardson's denunciation of both Pope and Swift.

131. Chapman, R. W. "Crousaz on Pope," *RES*, n.s., I (1950), 57.

Briefly states that Johnson's translation of Crousaz' *A Commentary on Mr. Pope's Principles of Morality* (1742) was actually a reissue of a rare edition printed by Cave in 1739. Chapman explains the possible reason for the reissue by citing Curll's 1738 publication of his *Commentary upon Mr. Pope's Four Ethic Epistles*.

132. Clark, Donald B. "The Italian Fame of Alexander Pope," *MLQ*, XXII (1961), 357–66.

Provides an account of Pope's critical prestige and of the translations of his works into Italian. Clark concludes that "Pope's reputation was not grounded upon his greatness as an artist; rather it was an interest in his subject matter that established him as the most widely read English poet in Italy" (p. 366).

133. Davies, Hugh S. (ed.). *The Poets and Their Critics: Chaucer to Collins.* 2d ed. London: Hutchinson Educational, 1960.

Includes excerpts of Pope criticism from the eighteenth to the early twentieth centuries.

134. Erdman, David V. "Byron and 'The New Force of the People,'" *Keats-Shelley Journal*, XI (1962), 47–64.

Provides an account of Byron's defense of Pope.

135. Fineman, Daniel A. "The Case of the Lady 'Killed' by Alexander Pope," *MLQ*, XII (1951), 137–49.

Identifies the text by Welsted (*Of Dulness and Scandal* [1732]) which explicitly accused Pope of "having 'killed' a lady (Sir Peter Vandeput's wife, Lady Frances) by *forcing her to read his translation of Homer's Iliad*" (p. 143). Fineman concludes that although the text bearing the charge, the "nature, motive and method of the 'crime,' and the victim have been discovered, the truth or falsity of Welsted's ironical accusation remains uncertain" (p. 149).

136. Hardy, John. "Stockdale's Defense of Pope," *RES*, n.s., XVIII (1967), 49–54.

Discusses Percival Stockdale's *Inquiry into the Nature and Genuine Laws of Poetry; including a Particular Defense of the Writings and Genius of Mr. Pope*, which was an effective reply to Joseph Warton's *Essay on the Writings and Genius of Pope*.

137. Hart, Jeffrey P. "Burke and Pope on Christianity," *Burke Newsletter*, vol. VII, no. 3 (Spring, 1967), pp. 702–13.

Prints a character-portrait of Pope written by Lord Chesterfield. The print "throws light on Pope's religious belief, at least insofar as he chose to reveal it to Chester-field."

138. *Honoré, Jean. "Charles Gildon rédacteur du *British Mercury* (1711–1712) : les attaques contre Pope, Swift, et les Wits," *EA*, xv (1962), 347–64.

139. Howard, Leon. "The American Revolt Against Pope," *SP*, XLIX (1952), 48–65.

> Explains that eighteenth-century American poets did not criticize Pope's style, but they did deny the "anti-theological" doctrine of *Essay on Man*. Howard also states that the early nineteenth-century revolt against the essay was "an attitude of reaction against passivity and toward an explicit faith in man's ability to control his future" (p. 56).

140. Jones, William Powell (ed.). *Sawney and Colley (1742) and Other Pope Pamphlets*. Augustan Reprint Society, no. 83. Los Angeles: University of California, 1960.

> Reproduces copies of two attacks on Pope: anonymous verses entitled "Sawney and Colley" and "Tit for Tat." In his introduction to the reprints, Jones suggests that the 1742 quarrel with Cibber occasioned ridicule for Pope's physical defects.

141. Kinghorn, A. M. "Warton's History and Early English Poetry," *ES*, XLIV (June, 1963), 197-204.

> Explains that Thomas Warton, who favored an historical approach to poetry, rejected Pope's "plans of classifying poetry into types."

142. Kinsley, J. "The Publication of Warton's *Essay on Pope*," *MLR*, XLIV (1949), 91–93.

> Examines the reason why the second volume of Joseph Warton's *Essay on Pope* was delayed for twenty-six years. Kinsley concludes that Warton did not want to jeopardize his advancement in church "by an over-violent criticism of Pope" (p. 93).

143. Leedy, Paul F. "Genres Criticism and the Significance of Warton's *Essay on Pope*," *JEGP*, XLV (1946), 140–46.

Maintains that although Joseph Warton's criticism (*Essay on the Genius and Writings of Pope*) was anticipated by Pope's early biographers, Warton's essay, which insisted upon the importance of imagination and invention, helped "to establish the fundamental cleavage between classicism and romanticism" (p. 145).

144. Loomis, Emerson Robert. "The Turning Point in Pope's Reputation: A Dispute Which Preceded the Bowles-Byron Controversy," *PQ*, XLII (1963), 242–48.

Describes the pamphlets of Mathias-Burdon which are significant in that they are the last critical statements which represent Pope as a first-rate poet, before the publication of *Lyrical Ballads*.

145. Mabbott, Thomas O. "An Intentional Parody of Pope by Crabbe," *N&Q*, CXCIX (1954), 525.

Indicates that four lines which appeared in Crabbe's poem "The Newspaper," later canceled by the poet but then "reprinted in the footnotes of the editions edited by his son," are a deliberate parody of *Essay on Criticism*, II, 370–73.

146. MacDonald, Wilbert Lorne. *Pope and His Critics: A Study in Eighteenth Century Personalities*. London: Dent, 1951.

Analyzes the critical and personal relationships of Pope and the criticisms of Ruffhead, Johnson, and Joseph Warton; focuses on the history of Popean criticism (and the possible basis for such criticism); and discusses the chief critical attitudes toward Pope during his own lifetime.

Reviewed by Clarence Tracy, *QQ*, LIX (1953), 124–26; Burns Martin, *DR*, XXXI (1951), xi–xiii; John Robert Moore, *MLN*, LXVIII (1953), 434–35; Douglas Knight, *MLQ*, XV (1954), 184–85.

147. Mahoney, John L. "Byron's Admiration of Pope: A Romantic Paradox," *Discourse*, V (1962), 309–15.

Provides a historical account of Byron's defense of and admiration for Pope's poetical merits and concludes that Byron's "admiration seldom extended beyond the realm of theory" (p. 314).

148. Marshall, William H. "Some Byron Comments on Pope and Boileau," *PQ*, XXXVIII (1959), 252–53.

Provides a copy (previously unpublished) of comments made by Byron concerning a comparison of Pope and Boileau written "during or after 1819 in the opening pages of the second volume of his own two-volume copy of Boileau's *Œuvres*" (p. 252). Marshall states that the comments tend to reflect "Byron's conscious appreciation of Pope" (p. 252).

149. Montague, Gene B. "The Queen Anne Revival." Unpublished Ph.D. dissertation, University of Texas, 1957, *DA*, XVII (1957), 2597.

Reviews the history of critical opinion of the eighteenth century from the hostile view of early Victorians such as Macaulay and Carlyle to the more favorable critics such as Austin Dobson, Edmund Gosse, and George Saintsbury, who helped stimulate public interest in Augustan writing.

150. Murray, Byron D. "Lowell's Criticism of Dryden and Pope," *State University of Iowa Doctoral Dissertations, Abstracts and References,* VI (1945), 434–41.

Studies major critical treatises on Pope and Dryden before Lowell's critical essays, examines how Lowell used such sources, and compares representative twentieth-century criticism of Pope and Dryden with Lowell's criticism. Murray concludes that Lowell's criticism of Dryden and Pope is effective and comprehensive.

151. Pafford, J. H. P. "Donne: An Early Nineteenth Century Estimate," *N&Q*, CCIV (1959), 131–32.

Reprints a criticism of Pope, Cowper, and Donne found in *Pieces of Ancient Poetry, from Unpublished Manuscripts and Scarce Books*, compiled by John Fry in 1814. Fry stated "that Pope was induced to modernise his Satires, from motives which, although neither honourable to his candour or his love of truth, were quite distinct from any belief in their merit" (p. 131).

152. Peterson, William M. "Pope and Cibber's *The Non-Juror*," *MLN*, LXX (1955), 332–35.

Cites Cibber's three satirical references to Pope's works in his play *The Non-Juror*. Peterson states that Cibber employed the same satirical device in his play as Pope had utilized in *Three Hours after Marriage*.

153. Pittock, Joan. "Joseph Warton and His Second Volume of the *Essay on Pope*," *RES*, n.s., XVIII (1967), 264–73.

Cites new evidence in order to explain Warton's twenty-six-year delay in publishing his *Essay on Pope*. Pittock concludes that the reasons "are traceable to the mixture of caution, ambition, and lack of time for or interest in the work to be completed . . ." (pp. 272–73).

154. Ryley, Robert Michael. "William Warburton as Critic and Editor of Pope." Unpublished Ph.D. dissertation, University of Minnesota, 1966, *DA*, XXVIII (1967), 642.

Collects and reinterprets the scattered material on "Warburton's defense of the *Essay on Man* . . . his editorial methods in the edition of Pope . . . the criticism in the edition of Pope, and . . . on his part in Ruffhead's *Life of Pope*."

155. Sackett, S. J. "Fielding and Pope," *N&Q*, CCIV (1959), 200–204.

Traces Fielding's respect, complimentary praise, and, finally, adverse criticism of Pope's works, especially the latter's translation of Homer.

156. Sambrook, A. J. (ed.). *The Scribleriad, Anonymous (1742); The Difference Between Verbal And Practical Virtue, Lord John Hervey*. Augustan Reprint Society, no. 125. Los Angeles: Clark Memorial Library, University of California, 1967.

Reprints the *Scribleriad*, Hervey's verses, and the "notorious *Letter from Mr. Cibber to Mr. Pope*" in order to reveal a Grub-Street-like defense of Pope and a court attack on Pope. Sambrook's introduction briefly examines the historical background of all three reprints.

157. *Sen, Sailendra Kumar. "Joseph Warton and the Romantic Heresy that Pope Was Not a Poet," *Bulletin of the Department of English, University of Calcutta*, II (no date), 33–37.

158. Shudofsky, Maurice M. "A Dunce Objects to Pope's Dictatorship," *HLQ*, XIV (1951), 203–7.

States that Charles Johnson retaliated for being "sneered" at by Pope. Shudofsky cites Johnson's critical preface to his play *Medea* (1731) and concludes that "it reminds us once more of Pope's abnormal vanity, [and] his brutal vengefulness" (p. 207).

159. Sibley, Agnes Marie. *Alexander Pope's Prestige in America, 1725-1835*. New York: Columbia University Press, 1949.

Employing representative American periodicals and newspapers during 1725 to 1835, Sibley considers the "philosophic, moral, and aesthetic aspects" (p. ix) of Pope's poetry as it influenced the reading, ideas, and criticism of the American public. A feature of Sibley's appendices is the listing of the date, place, and publisher of 160 editions of *Essay on Man* (plus editions of Pope's other works) and the location of copies in American libraries.

Reviewed by Robert W. Rogers, *PQ*, XXIX (1950), 292–93; Harry Hayden Clark, *American Literature*, XXXIII (1950), 141–42; John O. Eidson, *MLN*, LXVI (1951), 133–34.

160. Spector, Robert Donald. "Pope's Reputation as a Deist," *N&Q*, CXCVII (1952), 318.

Discusses Edmund Curll's attempt to discredit Pope's religious orthodoxy in relationship to the 1736 edition of *Essay on Human Life*, by Thomas Catesby, Lord Paget, which purported to have been written by Pope, but which was excluded from Warburton's edition because it contained passages pertaining to the "doctrine of fatality."

161. Wimsatt, William Kurtz, Jr., and Beardsley, M. C. "The Affective Fallacy," *SR*, LVII (1949), 31–55.

Contains a brief reference to Warton's *Essay on the Genius and Writings of Pope.*

GENERAL CRITICISM

162. Adelsberger, Sister Agnes Stephen. "Nature as Unifying Principle Underlying Aesthetic and Moral Judgments in the Works of Alexander Pope." Unpublished Ph.D. dissertation, University of Notre Dame, 1966, *DA*, XXVII (1967), 3418.

> Studies Pope's concept of nature as reflected in judgments made in Pope's satires; defines the concept and reveals how victims of Pope's satires were punished because they failed to follow his concept.

163. Anderson, Howard; Daghlian, Philip B.; and Ehrenpreis, Irvin (eds.). *The Familiar Letter in the Eighteenth Century*. Lawrence: University of Kansas Press, 1966.

> Contains the following essay: "Shadow and Substance: A Discussion of Pope's Correspondence," by Rosemary Elizabeth Cowler (653).

164. Auden, W. H. "Alexander Pope," *EIC*, I (1951), 208–24.

> Reprinted from *From Anne to Victoria: Essays by Various Hands* (1937). Contains a discussion of the political, social, economic, and intellectual climate of the eighteenth century; a brief biographical sketch; and an analysis of Pope's poetic diction. See also 219.

165. Ault, Norman. *New Light on Pope, with Some Additions to His Poetry Hitherto Unknown*. London: Methuen, 1949.

> Considers biographical incidents such as Pope's involvement with Lintot's *Miscellany*; discusses discoveries of variant texts of poems or parts of poems in Pope's canon; presents new evidence about existing poems in the canon; suggests that "the majority of Pope's unacknowledged pieces were written in metres other than the heroic couplet" (p. 11); and observes that the concealment of Pope's editorship and authorship was carried on extensively. See also 37, 41, and 597.
>
> Reviewed by Maynard Mack, *PQ*, XXIX (1950), 289–91; *TLS*, November 4, 1949, pp. 705–7; George Sherburn, *RES*,

n.s., II (1951), 84–86; Edith Sitwell, *Sunday Times* (London), October 2, 1949, p. 3.

166. Battestin, Martin C. "Lord Hervey's Role in *Joseph Andrews*," *PQ*, XLII (1963), 226–41.

Examines Fielding's use of Pope's satiric attacks on Hervey, discusses Fielding's and Pope's friendship and exchange of flattery, and notes Pope's references to Fielding's plays.

167. *Beck, Richard. *Jón Porláksson, Icelandic Translator of Pope and Milton*. Reykjavík: Leiftur, 1957.

168. Beers, Henry A. *A History of English Romanticism in the Eighteenth Century*. New York: Gordian Press, 1966.

Originally published in 1898, this work contains a chapter entitled "The School of Warton," which discusses Joseph Warton's relationship to Pope. Throughout the work, Beers makes references *passim* to Pope and his poetry.

169. Beljame, Alexandre. *Men of Letters and the English Public in the Eighteenth Century: 1660–1744, Dryden, Addison, Pope*. Edited by Bonamy Dobrée; translated by E. O. Lorimer. London: Kegan Paul, Trench, Trubner, 1948.

In chapter four, part IV, Beljame describes Pope's collaboration with Tonson and Lintot and the publication of Pope's translations of Homer, with emphasis on the significance of the dedication to the *Iliad*, and notes that Pope was the first real English man of letters since he refused political or social patronage. Part V deals with the injustices Pope has received at the hands of his biographers.

170. *Blanshard, Rufus A. (ed.). *Discussions of Alexander Pope*. Boston: Heath, 1960.

171. Blum, Margaret Morton. "Allen Tate's 'Mr. Pope': A Reading," *MLN*, LXXIV (1959), 706–8.

Explicates the title poem from Tate's collection, *Mr. Pope and Other Poems*, and states that the poem represents "Mr. Tate's effort to aid in the reëstablishment to popular esteem of a much-maligned poet" (p. 706).

172. Boys, Richard C. (ed.). *Studies in the Literature of the Augustan Age: Essays Collected in Honor of Arthur Ellicott Case*. New York: Gordian Press, 1966.

Contains the following essay: William Kurtz Wimsatt, Jr., "One Relation of Rhyme to Reason: Alexander Pope" (315).

173. Bredvold, Louis I. "The Gloom of the Tory Satirists," *Pope and His Contemporaries: Essays Presented to George Sherburn*. Edited by James L. Clifford and Louis A. Landa. Oxford: Clarendon Press, 1949.

Discusses the political, sociological, and moral climate of England as it influenced the satirical writings of Swift and Pope and suggests that both poets "had firm faith in the ultimate right order of things" (p. 4), while directing their attention to the problems of man in relationship to his society, rather than the problems of religion or philosophy. See also 185.

174. Brower, Reuben Arthur. "An Allusion to Europe: Dryden and Poetic Tradition," *Essential Articles for the Study of Alexander Pope*. Edited by Maynard Mack. Hamden, Conn.: Shoestring Press, 1964.

Traces in detail the European (ancient and contemporary) literary traditions of Dryden's "allusive," satirical mode and substantiates the contention that Pope was influenced by the allusive-satirical mode and self-parody of Dryden's poetical tradition. See also 219 and 272.

175. ———. "Dryden and the 'Invention' of Pope," *Restoration and Eighteenth-Century Literature. Essays in Honor of Alan Dugald McKillop*. Edited by Carroll Camden. Chicago: University of Chicago Press for William Marsh Rice University, 1963.

Examines "some of the ways in which Dryden's poetry from about 1685 until his death anticipated Pope," in Dryden's Horatian, pastoral, and descriptive style and in his "poetry of retirement." See also 182.

176. Brückmann, Patricia Laureen. "Allusions to Pope," *UTQ*, XXXIII (1964), 227–32.

Lists and comments on recent (1959–1962) critical scholarship on Pope: *Pastoral Poetry and An Essay on Criticism*, edited by E. Audra and Aubrey L. Williams (1); Reuben Arthur Brower's *Alexander Pope: The Poetry of Allusion* (272); *The Character-Sketches in Pope's Poems*, by Benjamin Boyce (270); and Earl R. Wasserman's *Pope's Epistle to Bathurst: A Critical Reading with an Edition of the Manuscripts* (491).

177. Butt, John. *The Augustan Age*. London: Hutchinson, 1950.

Chapter five contains a general interpretative discussion of Pope's works.

178. ———. "The Inspiration of Pope's Poetry," *Essays on the Eighteenth Century Presented to David Nichol Smith in Honour of His Seventieth Birthday*. Oxford: Clarendon Press, 1945.

Contains a general discussion of Pope's methods in describing and in generalizing character-portraits. Butt focuses on Pope's "ethical and topical" inspiration as it is directed toward "improving the existing social state" (p. 68) and concludes that Pope's inspirations were "drawn from fancy, morality, and books" (p. 77).

Reviewed by Maynard Mack, *PQ*, xxv (1946), 158–61.

179. ——— (ed.). *Of Books and Humankind: Essays and Poems Presented to Bonamy Dobrée*. Assisted by J. M. Cameron, D. W. Jefferson, and Robin Skelton. London: Routledge & Kegan Paul, 1964.

Contains the following essay: John Butt, "Pope: The Man and the Poet" (180).

180. ———. "Pope: The Man and the Poet," *Of Books and Humankind: Essays and Poems Presented to Bonamy Dobrée*. Edited by John Butt and assisted by J. M. Cameron, D. W. Jefferson, and Robin Skelton. London: Routledge & Kegan Paul, 1964.

In his biographical-general interpretative essay, Butt sees Pope's persona as an enigma between the historical and the literary portrait. See also 179.

181. Callan, Norman. "Alexander Pope," *From Dryden to Johnson*. The Pelican Guide to English Literature, edited by Boris Ford, vol. IV. Baltimore: Penguin Books, 1957.

> States that Pope was "the poet of his age" and a spokesman for his society; comments on the nature and purpose of Popean imitation of earlier poetry; and provides a general discussion of *Rape of the Lock*, the *Dunciad*, and *Essay on Criticism*.

182. Camden, Carroll (ed.). *Restoration and Eighteenth-Century Literature. Essays in Honor of Alan Dugald McKillop*, Chicago: University of Chicago Press for William Marsh Rice University, 1963.

> Consists of the following essays: " 'The Shadowy Cave': Some Speculations on a Twickenham Grotto," by Maynard Mack (221); "Mr. Pope, in Bath, Improves the Design of His Grotto," by Benjamin Boyce (44); "Dryden and the 'Invention' of Pope," by Reuben Arthur Brower (175); "The Methods of Description in Eighteenth- and Nineteenth-Century Poetry," by Geoffrey Tillotson (308); "Pope and Horace: *The Second Epistle of the Second Book*," by Aubrey L. Williams (533); and " 'Amicitiae Causa': A Birthday Present from Curll to Pope," by William Kurtz Wimsatt, Jr. (674).

183. Clark, Donald B. *Alexander Pope*. Twayne's English Authors Series. New York: Twayne Publishers, 1967.

> Interprets Pope's major works placing emphasis on Pope's "vision of harmony through variety" and states that Pope's employment of allusion and metaphor are key factors in his development as a poet.

184. Clifford, James L. "The Eighteenth Century," *MLQ*, XXVI (1965), 111–34.

> In an attempt to assess twenty-five years of eighteenth-century scholarship, Clifford finds an "emphasis on careful and thorough scholarship" and a double approach to interpretation: "first, in relation to the basic ideas of the eighteenth-century; and then in the context . . . of modern critical theory" (p. 134).

185. ———— (ed.). *Eighteenth-Century English Literature: Modern Essays in Criticism*. New York: Oxford University Press, 1959.

Consists of the following essays: "The Gloom of the
Tory Satirists," by Louis I. Bredvold (173); "'Wit and
Poetry and Pope': Some Observations on His Imagery,"
by Maynard Mack (295); "Pope on Wit: The *Essay on
Criticism*," by Edward Niles Hooker (342); "Pope Seen
Through His Letters," by John Butt (651); "The Back-
ground of the Attack on Science in the Age of Pope," by
Richard Foster Jones (214); and "Eighteenth-Century
Poetic Diction," by Geoffrey Tillotson (307).

186. Clifford, James L., and Landa, Louis A. (eds.). *Pope and
His Contemporaries: Essays Presented to George Sherburn.*
Oxford: Clarendon Press, 1949.

Consists of the following essays: John Butt's "A Master
Key to Popery" (478); Geoffrey Tillotson's "Pope's *Epistle
to Harley*: An Analysis" (613); Louis I. Bredvold's "The
Gloom of the Tory Satirists" (173); Maynard Mack's "'Wit
and Poetry and Pope': Some Observations on His Imagery"
(295); Robert J. Allen's "Pope and the Sister Arts" (261);
Arthur Friedman's "Pope and Deism" (551); Richard F.
Jones' "The Background of the Attack on Science in the
Age of Pope" (214); and Joseph Wood Krutch's "Pope
and Our Contemporaries" (217).

Reviewed by Delancey Ferguson, *NYHTBR*, April 16,
1950, p. 12; *N&Q*, cxcv (1950), 264; Robert Halsband,
SatR, July 8, 1950, p. 17; R. S. Crane, *YR*, xxxix (1949),
753–55; William Henry Irving, *SAQ*, L (1951), 289; *TLS*,
February 10, 1950, p. 87; Norman Callan, *RES*, n.s., II
(1951), 389–91.

187. Cox, Carrol Byron, Jr. "Pope in the Twentieth Century."
Unpublished Ph.D. dissertation, University of Michigan,
1964, *DA*, xxv (1965), 7263–64.

Identifies twentieth-century views of Pope's poetry and
relates "those views both to one another and to views prevailing at the end of the nineteenth-century." Cox focuses
on criticism from Austin Warren's *Alexander Pope as
Critic and Humanist* (1929) to Maynard Mack's introduction to *Essay on Man* (1950).

188. Cruttwell, Patrick. "Alexander Pope in the Augustan
World," *CentR*, x (1966), 13–36.

Suggests that Pope's elite friends who were his "image
of the ideal community" can be grouped as "The Wits,"

"The Country," and "The Lords." Cruttwell analyzes Pope's relationship to his friends and his function in Augustan England and concludes that Pope, through his poetry, sincerely endeavored "to please and to instruct."

189. *Curtis, Penelope. "Pope the Good Augustan," *MCR*, VII (1964), 34–48.

190. De Selincourt, Aubrey. "Alexander Pope," *Six Great Poets*. London: Hamish Hamilton, 1956.

Discusses the general historical climate of the early eighteenth century, with emphasis on why Pope was not an innovator, why the London "wits" employed the Latin classics as models, and why the Augustans were concerned with "man as a social being" as the central theme of their poetry. De Selincourt's chapter on Pope (pp. 41–80) includes a biography of the poet and a general explication of the *Pastorals, Essay on Criticism, Rape of the Lock, Dunciad,* and Pope's translation of the *Iliad.*

Reviewed by James Reeves, *Observer*, March 11, 1956, p. 17.

191. *De Stasio, Clotilde. "Pope, Berkeley e il *Guardian,*" *Acme*, XIX (1966), 341–58.

192. Dobrée, Bonamy. *English Literature in the Early Eighteenth Century, 1700–1740.* Oxford History of English Literature, edited by F. P. Wilson and Bonamy Dobrée, vol. 7. Oxford: Clarendon Press, 1959.

Contains two chapters on Pope: "Pope to 1725" and "Pope, 1725–1744." The former contains a brief biography and a general explication of *Windsor Forest, Essay on Criticism, Rape of the Lock, Temple of Fame,* the minor poems, and Pope's translation of Homer. The latter chapter provides an analysis of the *Dunciad* and *Essay on Man.*

193. Eastman, Arthur M. "The Quality of Mercy: A Reply to Pope's Apologists," *PMASAL*, XLIII (1957), 335–42.

States that a distinction must be made between Pope as a person and his persona and maintains that Pope's apologists must teach their students that Pope's aesthetic satire is moral; consequently, moral judgment should be applied to his satires.

194. *Eddy, Donald D. "A New Note from Pope," *Cornell Library Journal,* III (1967), 56–57.

195. Edwards, Thomas Robert, Jr. "Pope's Versions of Nature: The Progression from 'Neo-Classic' to 'Grotesque' Poetic Style." Unpublished Ph.D. dissertation, Harvard University, 1956.

> Examines "Pope's major poems . . . interpreting the ways in which they express varying and developing views of the relation of human experience . . . to the non-human world of 'nature'" (p. viii). Edwards also provides a detailed analysis of Pope's language and themes in order to study his poetic style.

196. ———. *This Dark Estate: A Reading of Pope.* Perspectives in Criticism, no. 11. Berkeley: University of California Press, 1963.

> Provides a general interpretative study of all Pope's major works, with the exception of his translations and literary criticism.
>
> Reviewed by Geoffrey Bullough, *English,* XIV (1963), 200–202; Hoyt Trowbridge, *PQ,* XLIII (1964), 377–78; Aubrey L. Williams, *JEGP,* LXIV (1965), 319–22.

197. *Ehrenpreis, Irvin. "The Cistern and the Fountain: Art and Reality in Pope and Gray," *Studies in Criticism and Aesthetics, 1660–1800: Essays in Honor of Samuel Holt Monk.* Edited by Howard Anderson and John S. Shea. Minneapolis: University of Minnesota Press, 1967.

198. *Feder, Lillian. "Sermon or Satire: Pope's Definition of His Art," *Studies in Criticism and Aesthetics, 1660–1800: Essays in Honor of Samuel Holt Monk.* Edited by Howard Anderson and John S. Shea. Minneapolis: University of Minnesota Press, 1967.

199. Felps, Jettie Irving. *Pope's Common Sense.* Boston: Meador, 1958.

> Maintains that "Pope showed a very consistent common sense not only in his life, his life's ideals, his friendships,

his religion, and his dealings with his enemies, but also in his letters and in his poetry" (p. 8).

200. Frost, William. "Recent Studies in the Restoration and Eighteenth Century," *SEL*, II (1962), 359–84.

> Lists the following studies on Pope: Maynard Mack's "The Muse of Satire" (294); Joseph S. Cunningham's *Pope: The Rape of the Lock* (376); and E. Audra's and Aubrey L. Williams' edition of Pope's *Pastoral Poetry and An Essay on Criticism* (1).

201. Gilmore, Thomas B. "Colley Cibber's Good Nature and His Reaction to Pope's Satire," *PLL*, II (1966), 361–71.

> Argues against the "uncritical and sometimes undeserved praise bestowed on Cibber for his good-natured treatment of Pope." Gilmore substantiates his contention by demonstrating "the distinct and numerous similarities between [Cibber's] reactions and those of other dunces" (p. 371).

202. *Goldberg, S. L. "Alexander Pope," *MCR*, VII (1964), 49–65.

203. Graves, Robert. *The Crowning Privilege*. New York: Doubleday, 1956.

> Contains a brief biographical sketch and general commentary on Pope's "technical incompetency" (p. 45).

204. *Greany, Helen T. "Satiric Masks: Swift and Pope," *SNL*, III (1966), 154–59.

205. Gregory, Horace. "The Double Vision in Pope's Poetry," *Poetry*, LXXVII (1951), 340–50.

> Reviews *The Pleasures of Pope*, edited by Peter Quennell (see 18), and provides a biographical-interpretative sketch of Pope and some of his poetry.

206. Grierson, Herbert J. C., and Smith, J. C. *A Critical History of English Poetry*. London: Chatto & Windus, 1947.

> Chapter sixteen, "The Age of Pope and Other Augustans,"

contains a brief biographical sketch and a general interpretative discussion of Pope's works.

207. Halsband, Robert. "Eighteenth-Century Savant," *SatR*, xxxv (May 3, 1952), 19–20.

States that a revival of interest in Pope is reflected in the Twickenham Edition of his works and in recent publications dealing with Pope and his poetry.

208. Harrison, G. B. (ed.). *Major British Writers*, vol. I. New York: Harcourt, Brace, 1954.

Contains an extensive selection of Pope's poetry. The section on Pope is prefaced by a biographical-interpretative study of Pope and his works written by Maynard Mack. Each of the selections is preceded by Mack's commentary on its background and composition and by a general interpretation of the work. (This work is published as a text for sophomore literature courses.)

209. Hilles, Frederick W., and Bloom, Harold (eds.). *From Sensibility to Romanticism: Essays Presented to Frederick A. Pottle*. New York: Oxford University Press, 1965.

Contains the following essays: Maynard Mack's "A Poet in His Landscape: Pope at Twickenham" (61); Donald J. Greene's "Dramatic Texture in Pope" (282); and William Kurtz Wimsatt, Jr.'s "An Image of Pope" (73). See also 234.

210. Huseboe, Arthur Robert. "Alexander Pope's Dramatic Imagination." Unpublished Ph.D. dissertation, Indiana University, 1964, *DA*, xxiv (1964), 2891–92.

Deals with "Pope's relation to dramatic art"; Pope's extended quarrels with men associated with drama; his interest in and attendance at stage productions; and how Pope's "career-long" interest in drama influenced the theme or structure of *Peri Bathous*, the *Dunciad*, *Epistle to Augustus*, *Rape of the Lock*, *Eloisa to Abelard*, and *Verses to the Memory of an Unfortunate Lady*.

211. Jack, Ian. *Pope*. Bibliographical Series of Supplements to the British Book News, no. 48. London: Longmans, Green, 1954.

Provides a brief (27 pp.) biographical-interpretative sketch of Pope and of the following works: *Windsor Forest, Rape of the Lock, Epistle to Dr. Arbuthnot,* and the *Dunciad.* Jack also includes a selective bibliography of collected editions of Pope's works, biographies, and criticism.

212. Johnson, James William. *The Formation of English Neo-Classical Thought.* Princeton: Princeton University Press, 1967.

Makes an extensive number of brief comments regarding Pope in relationship to the "prevailing twentieth century critical understanding of English Neo-Classicism" (p. x).

213. Johnston, Arthur. " 'The Purple Year' in Pope and Gray," *RES,* n.s., XIV (1963), 389–93.

Traces Pope's employment of "the purple year" to Virgil, Dryden, and especially to the *Pervigilium Veneris.* Johnston also provides detailed instances of use of the phrase by English and Latin poets.

214. Jones, Richard Foster. "The Background of the Attack on Science in the Age of Pope," *Pope and His Contemporaries: Essays Presented to George Sherburn.* Edited by James L. Clifford and Louis A. Landa. Oxford: Clarendon Press, 1949.

Suggests the possible grounds for eighteenth-century satire against science by analyzing "the unique features of the opposition to experimental science in the second half of the seventeenth century" (p. 68). See also 185 and 186.

215. ———. *The Seventeenth Century: Studies in the History of English Thought and Literature from Bacon to Pope.* Stanford: Stanford University Press, 1951.

Contains a series of essays by Jones and other writers, including Edward N. Hooker's "Pope on Wit: the *Essay on Criticism*" (342); and George Sherburn's "Pope and 'The Great Shew of Nature'" (239).

Reviewed by Donald M. Foerster, *PQ,* XXXI (1952), 288; *TLS,* February 22, 1952, p. 143.

216. Knight, G. Wilson. *Laureate of Peace: On the Genius of Alexander Pope.* New York: Oxford University Press, 1955.

This book is divided into the following five sections: (1) a brief general survey of Pope's doctrine and diction; (2) "an interpretative study" of *Windsor Forest, Rape of the Lock, Eloisa to Abelard, Essay on Man,* the *Dunciad,* and *Moral Essays,* which is a "slightly" revised version of "The Vital Flame" first published in Knight's *The Burning Oracle* (1939); (3) an analysis of the *Temple of Fame*; (4) a discussion of "Byron's adulation of Pope"; and (5) a description of "Pope's poetic thought in relation to our own time" (p. viii). See also 476.

Reviewed in *TLS,* December 31, 1954, p. 850; answered by G. Wilson Knight, *TLS,* January 14, 1955, p. 25; Hoyt Trowbridge, *PQ,* xxxv (1956), 318–19; Norman Callan, *RES*, n.s., VIII (1957), 96–97; Mario Praz, *ES,* XXXVIII (1957), 84–90.

217. Krutch, Joseph Wood. "Pope and Our Contemporaries," *Pope and His Contemporaries: Essays Presented to George Sherburn.* Edited by James L. Clifford and Louis A. Landa. Oxford: Clarendon Press, 1949.

Suggests the reasons why Pope does not make a strong appeal to contemporary audiences and discusses the tradition Pope inherited from Dryden. See also 186.

218. Levine, Jay Arnold. "The Status of the Verse Epistle Before Pope," *SP,* LIX (1962), 658–84.

Examines seventeenth- and eighteenth-century practitioners of the verse epistle, studies "the theory and practice which anticipated—or fostered—Pope's conception" (p. 661) of the verse epistle, and concludes that Pope's "full adherence to the rhetorical mode was not without precedent" (p. 684).

219. Mack, Maynard (ed.). *Essential Articles for the Study of Alexander Pope.* Hamden, Conn.: Shoestring Press, 1964.

Reprints the following forty-four articles: F. R. Leavis, "Pope" (292); W. H. Auden, "Alexander Pope" (164); Samuel Holt Monk, "A Grace Beyond the Reach of Art" (349); William Kurtz Wimsatt, Jr., "One Relation of Rhyme to Reason: Alexander Pope" (315); Austin Warren, "Pope" (331); Frederick Bracher, "Pope's Grotto: The Maze of Fancy" (46); Reuben Arthur Brower, "An Allusion to Europe: Dryden and Poetic Tradition" (174); A. Lynn Alten-

bernd, "On Pope's 'Horticultural Romanticism' " (477); Earl
R. Wasserman, "Pope's *Ode for Musick*" (616); Edward
Niles Hooker, "Pope on Wit: The *Essay on Criticism*" (342);
William Empson, "Wit in the *Essay on Criticism*" (338); Ar-
thur Fenner, Jr., "The Unity of Pope's *Essay on Criticism*"
(339); John Robert Moore, "*Windsor Forest* and William
III" (324); Cleanth Brooks, "The Case of Miss Arabella
Fermor: A Re-examination" (367); William Frost, "*The
Rape of the Lock* and Pope's Homer" (379); Aubrey L.
Williams, "The 'Fall' of China and *The Rape of the Lock*"
(411); Rebecca Price Parkin, "Tension in Alexander Pope's
Poetry" (394); Henry Pettit, "Pope's *Eloisa to Abelard*:
An Interpretation" (418); Brendan P. O'Hehir, "Virtue and
Passion: The Dialectic of *Eloisa to Abelard*" (417); J. M.
Cameron, "Doctrinal to an Age: Notes Towards a Revalua-
tion of Pope's *Essay on Man*" (426); Richard Edward
Hughes, "Pope's *Essay on Man*: The Rhetorical Structure
of Epistle I" (444); Robert W. Rogers, "Alexander Pope's
Universal Prayer" (603); Vinton A. Dearing, "The Prince
of Wales's Set of Pope's Works" (29); Ian Jack, "Pope
and 'The Weighty Bullion of Dr. Donne's Satires' " (519);
G. R. Hibbard, "The Country House Poem of the Seventeenth Century" (485); Paul J. Alpers, "Pope's *To Bathurst*
and the Mandevillian State" (476); Norman Ault, "Pope
and Addison" (41); Lillian D. Bloom, "Pope as Textual
Critic: A Bibliographical Study of His Horatian Text"
(506); John Butt, "Pope's Poetical Manuscripts" (27); Elias
F. Mengel, "Patterns of Imagery in Pope's *Arbuthnot*"
(502); James M. Osborn, "Pope, the Byzantine Empress,
and Walpole's Whore" (527); G. K. Hunter, "The 'Romanticism' of Pope's Horace" (518); John M. Aden, "Pope and
the Satiric Adversary" (505); Norman Callan, "Pope's
Iliad: A New Document" (619); Douglas Knight, "The Development of Pope's *Iliad* Preface: A Study of the Manuscript" (634); Robert M. Schmitz, "The 'Arsenal' Proof
Sheets of Pope's *Iliad*: A Third Report" (642); James R.
Sutherland, " 'The Dull Duty of an Editor' " (576); Donald
F. Bond, "The Importance of Pope's Letters" (649); Reginald Harvey Griffith, "*The Dunciad*" (553); George Sherburn, "*The Dunciad,* Book IV" (573); Hugo M. Reichard,
"Pope's Social Satire: Belles-Lettres and Business" (569);
Thomas Robert Edwards, "Light and Nature: A Reading
of the *Dunciad*" (547); Alvin B. Kernan, "The *Dunciad* and
the Plot of Satire" (559); Howard H. Erskine-Hill, "The
'New World' of Pope's *Dunciad*" (549).

220. Mack, Maynard. "Secretum Iter: Some Uses of Retire-

ment Literature in the Poetry of Pope," *Aspects of the Eighteenth Century.* Edited by Earl R. Wasserman. Baltimore: Johns Hopkins Press, 1965.

Studies the varied employment of the theme of solitude and retirement in the poetry of Pope. Mack also briefly comments on the theme of retirement, especially in the poetry of Cowley, Donne, and Marvell. See also 253.

221. Mack, Maynard. " 'The Shadowy Cave': Some Speculations on a Twickenham Grotto," *Restoration and Eighteenth-Century Literature. Essays in Honor of Alan Dugald McKillop.* Edited by Carroll Camden. Chicago: University of Chicago Press for William Marsh Rice University, 1963.

Examines the nature and employment of Pope's grotto as an "accessory to his Muse" and to his life. Mack states that "Pope's career . . . *was* determined by the effort to extract ornament from inconvenience . . ." (p. 78); and observes that Pope's grotto and garden provided Pope, the satirist, both "literally and figuratively, with a place to stand, an angle of vision" (p. 86). See also 182.

222. McKillop, Alan Dugald. *English Literature from Dryden to Burns.* New York: Appleton-Century-Crofts, 1948.

Provides a biographical account of Pope's life and brief interpretative studies of *Essay on Criticism, Rape of the Lock,* the *Dunciad,* and *Essay on Man.*

223. MacLure, Millar, and Watt, F. W. (eds.). *Essays in English Literature from the Renaissance to the Victorian Age Presented to A. S. P. Woodhouse.* Toronto: University of Toronto Press, 1964.

Contains the following essay: "Pope and the Great Chain of Being," by F. E. L. Priestley (462).

224. *Mahaffey, Lois Kathleen. "Timon's Villa: Walpole's Houghton," *TSLL,* IX (1967), 193–222.

225. Maxwell, J. C. " 'Classic,' " *N&Q,* CCVIII (1963), 220.

Corrects *OED* source for *classic* from *Imitations of*

Horace (1737) to George Sewell's preface to Pope's Shakespeare (1725).

226. Means, James A. "Three Notes on Pope," *N&Q*, XIV (1967), 410.

Suggests the following parallels: (1) *Dunciad*, III, 165–66, with Waller's *Of the Misreport of Her Being Painted*, 1–2; (2) Pope's *Spring*, 77–80, with Denham's translation of *Cato Major*, III, 187–90; (3) *Essay on Criticism*, II, 356-57, with Dryden's *Aeneid*, V, 359–66

227. Miller, John H. "Pope and the Principle of Reconciliation," *TSLL*, IX (1967), 185–92.

Pope's ability to "harmonize, conciliate, and reconcile differences" (p. 192) in politics and religion is examined in relationship to *Essay on Criticism, Rape of the Lock,* and *Windsor Forest.*

228. Monk, Samuel Holt. *The Sublime: A Study of Critical Theories in XVIII-Century England.* Ann Arbor: University of Michigan Press, 1960.

First published in 1935, this study makes references *passim* to Pope's relationship to Augustan critical theory.

229. Nierenberg, Edwin H. "Pope and God at Twickenham," *Personalist*, XLIV (1963), 472–89.

Studies Pope's religious system in reference to Pope's concept of immortality and briefly considers the orthodoxy of *Essay on Man* and *Elegy to the Memory of an Unfortunate Lady.* Nierenberg finds that "Pope eclectically and independently drew upon various systems and faiths in his attempt to achieve a vital synthesis" (p. 472) and that Pope "practised an ideal of moderation, proportion, and eclectic balance in religion" (p. 478).

230. Osborn, James M. "Addison's Tavern Companion and Pope's 'Umbra,' " *PQ*, XLII (1963), 217-25.

Establishes the identity and describes Walter Cary, a companion of Addison's "little Senate." Osborn substantiates his contention that Walter Cary is "the original of Pope's 'Umbra.' "

231. Petit, Herbert H. (ed.). *Essays and Studies in English Language and Literature.* Duquesne Studies—Philological Series, no. 5. Pittsburgh: Duquesne University Press, 1964.

Contains the following essay: "Pope's Defense of Theology, Philosophy, and the Arts in *Dunciad,* IV," by John W. Crowther, Jr. (543).

232. Potter, George R., and Butt, John. *Editing Donne and Pope.* Los Angeles: University of California Press, 1952.

The second article within this pamphlet ("Editorial Problems in Eighteenth-Century Poetry"), by John Butt, deals with the following problems in editing Pope's minor poems: the "problem of establishing the canon" (p. 11) and proving the authorship of anonymous poems "published in miscellanies edited by Pope" and "of poems to which Pope refers in uncertain terms in his letters or in his recorded conversations" (p. 13).

Reviewed in *TLS,* December 4, 1953, p. 790.

233. Price, Martin. "Pope: Art and Morality," *To the Palace of Wisdom: Studies in Order and Energy from Dryden to Blake.* Garden City, N.Y.: Doubleday, 1964.

In his chapter entitled "Pope: Art and Morality," Price deals with the relationship of Shaftesbury and Mandeville to Pope's *Essay on Man,* especially the third epistle; analyzes the "problem of scale" in Pope's *Pastorals* and *Rape of the Lock*; examines Pope's use of "the mock order of false art as a symbol of moral failure" (p. 155) in the *Moral Essays*; and discusses Pope's tone of morality in *Imitations of Horace.*

234. ———. "Recent Studies in the Restoration and Eighteenth Century," *SEL,* V (1965), 553–74.

Cites the following scholarship on Pope: *From Sensibility to Romanticism: Essays Presented to Frederick A. Pottle,* edited by Frederick W. Hilles and Harold Bloom. See 61, 73, 209, and 282.

235. *Rawlinson, David H. "Pope and Addison on Classical Greatness," *Wascana Review,* vol. II, no. 2 (1967), pp. 69–74.

236. Root, Robert Kilburn. *The Poetical Career of Alexander Pope*. Gloucester, Mass.: Peter Smith, 1962. (First printed in 1938 by the Princeton University Press.)

Analyzes in detail Pope's "sources of variation," intricate patterns, and methods in his use of the heroic couplet and explicates *Essay on Criticism, Pastorals, Rape of the Lock, Dunciad*, 1729 and 1743, *Essay on Man, Moral Essays*, and Pope's translations of Homer's *Iliad* and *Odyssey*.

237. *Røstvig, Maren-Sofie. *The Background of English Neo-Classicism, with Some Comments on Swift and Pope*. Oslo: Universitetsforl, 1961.

238. Secord, Arthur W. "Our Indispensable Eighteenth Century," *JEGP*, XLV (1946), 153–63.

Provides an account of recent scholarship pertaining to major eighteenth-century figures, specifically Pope. Secord focuses on modern criticism of Pope's major works and concludes that present critics tend to negate the nineteenth-century contempt for Pope's works.

239. Sherburn, George. "Pope and 'The Great Shew of Nature,' " *The Seventeenth Century: Studies in the History of English Thought and Literature from Bacon to Pope, by Richard Foster Jones and Others Writing in His Honor*. Stanford: Stanford University Press, 1951.

Discusses Pope's concept of nature, which as an ordered universe was "to be interpreted and understood especially in its relations to humanity" (p. 306); suggests the extent to which physical science influenced Pope's poetry; and substantiates Pope's reverence for Universal Nature. See also 215.

240. ———. "The Restoration and Eighteenth Century (1660–1789)," *A Literary History of England*. Edited by Albert C. Baugh. New York: Appleton-Century-Crofts, 1948.

Book III, part II, contains two sections on Pope. The first section relates to Pope as a critic, while the second contains a brief biography and a general discussion of Pope's minor poems, the *Rape of the Lock*, translation of Homer, edition

of Shakespeare, *Dunciad, Moral Essays, Essay on Man,* and
Imitations of Horace.

241. Simon, Irène. "Pope and the Fragility of Beauty," *Revue des Langues Vivantes,* XXIV (1958), 377–94.

>   Cites passages from Pope's works, especially *Essay on Man, Essay on Criticism, Rape of the Lock,* and the *Dunciad,* in order to establish Pope's awareness "of the fragility of beauty, whether natural or man made" (p. 379). Simon states that Pope was neither optimistic nor complacent about the precarious state of beauty.

242. Steensma, Robert C. "Swift on Standing Armies: A Possible Source," *N&Q,* CCVIII (1963), 215–16.

>   Passing reference is made to a Swift letter to Alexander Pope on the subject of standing armies.

243. *Stephen, Sir Leslie. *History of English Thought in the Eighteenth Century.* With a new preface by Crane Brinton. 4th ed. rev. Harcourt, Brace, & World, 1962.

244. Sutherland, James R. *A Preface to Eighteenth Century Poetry.* Oxford: Oxford University Press, 1948.

>   Contains critical references *passim* to Pope's artistry. Sutherland focuses on a discussion of what eighteenth-century "poets were doing and what they were not attempting to do" (p. iii) and considers why Augustan poetry differs from that of other periods.

245. Thomson, James A. K. *Classical Influences on English Poetry.* London: Allen & Unwin, 1951.

>   Briefly discusses Pope's translation of the *Iliad, Essay on Criticism, Messiah, Pastorals,* and *Imitations of Horace* and indicates that Pope was influenced by Homer, Horace, and Virgil.

246. Thornton, Francis Beauchesne. *Alexander Pope: Catholic Poet.* New York: Pellegrini & Cudahy, 1952.

>   Focuses on a biographical-interpretative study of Pope and his works (especially *Essay on Man*) in regard to the

influence of Catholic theology and the exponents of Catholic doctrine on Pope's poetry.

Reviewed by Sister Mary Frances, *Thought,* XXVIII (1952), 134–37; Robert Halsband, *SatR,* May 3, 1952, pp. 19–20.

247. Tillotson, Geoffrey. *The Moral Poetry of Pope.* Newcastle upon Tyne: Literary & Philosophical Society, 1946.

Studies Pope's concept of, and attitude toward, right and wrong. Tillotson comments on Pope's use of satire (in the *Dunciad*) in order to reveal the "antipathy" of good to bad writers, bad writing, and bad taste. Special emphasis is placed on a discussion of Pope's moral "scheme" or code as reflected in *Essay on Man* and the *Moral Essays*.

248. ———. "Poet of Plenitude," *Listener,* August 3, 1950, pp. 161, 164.

Provides a general discussion of Pope's preoccupation with "the plenitude of material things," with nature, and with man.

249. ———. *Pope and Human Nature.* Oxford: Clarendon Press, 1958.

Devotes the first four chapters to an explanation of the eighteenth-century concept of nature, human nature, and man's place in a personal, social, and moral context; discusses the varied "senses" of the terms *truth, just, judgment,* and *beauty* in chapters five through seven; deals with the concept of primary and secondary nature in relationship to mankind, the poet, and the critic in the next two chapters; and analyzes Pope's diction, rhetorical effects, the range of his imagery, the complexity of his couplets, and the appeal of his satiric poetry in the last two chapters. See also 336.

Reviewed by W. W. Robson, *Spectator,* October 3, 1958, p. 452; *TLS,* November 28, 1958, p. 690; Bertrand H. Bronson, *PQ,* XXXVIII (1959), 343–44; Richmond P. Bond, *MLR,* LIV (1959), 596–97; Emrys Jones, *CritQ,* I (1959), 173–75; Robert W. Rogers, *MP,* LVII (1959), 60–62; Bernhard Fabian, *Anglia,* LXXVII (1959), 359–62; William Frost, *MLN,* LXXV (1960), 53–56; G. K. Hunter, *RES,* n.s., XI (1960), 87–89.

250. *Tobin, James E. "Alexander Pope and the Classical Tradition," *Quarterly Bulletin of the Polish Institute,* III (1945), 343–53.

251. Trickett, Rachel. *The Honest Muse: A Study in Augustan Verse.* Oxford: Clarendon Press, 1967.

> Provides (in chapter six, pp. 156–223) a general interpretation of Pope's poetry; considers "some of the attitudes and assumptions" of Pope's poetry, which are studied "in relation to the political and intellectual circumstances" (p. vii) of his milieu. Trickett concludes that "Pope created a style in which the conventions of satire and the traditions of morality could merge with a new and introspective sensibility . . ." (p. 222).

252. Wain, John. *Essays on Literature and Ideas.* London: Macmillan, 1963.

> In his chapter entitled "An Introduction to Pope," Wain provides a general discussion of Pope and his poetry.

253. Wasserman, Earl R. (ed.). *Aspects of the Eighteenth Century.* Baltimore: Johns Hopkins Press, 1965.

> Contains the following essay: "Secretum Iter: Some Uses of Retirement Literature in the Poetry of Pope," by Maynard Mack (220).

254. Watson, Melvin R. "The *Spectator* Tradition and the Development of the Familiar Essay," *ELH,* XIII (1946), 189–215.

> Traces the tradition of the personal or familiar essay of the seventeenth century and contrasts its style with that of the social and moral essay of the eighteenth century. (Significant in view of Pope's authorship of essays in the *Guardian.*)

255. *Wellington, James E. "Pope's 'Alas! How Chang'd': Some Variations on a Vergilian Theme," *The Carrell: Journal of the Friends of the University of Miami (Fla.) Library,* vol. VII, no. 2 (1966), pp. 9–16.

256. Williams, T. G. *English Literature: A Critical Survey.* London: Sir Isaac Pitman & Sons, 1951.

> In the chapter entitled "Augustan Poetry," Williams briefly surveys Pope's major works and his use of the heroic couplet.

STYLE: POETICAL TECHNIQUES

257. Adams, Percy G. "Pope's Concern with Assonance," *TSLL*, IX (1968), 493–502.

Compares the "prosodic theories" of Pope and Dryden and studies Pope's use of assonance. Adams concludes that Pope's manipulation of assonance for parallelism, emphasis, sound, and balance was "sweet and pleasing," deliberate, and masterful.

258. Aden, John M. "Pope and the Receit to Make a Satire," *SNL*, V (1967), 25–33.

Sees "Pope's theory of satire [as] a correlative of his theory of human nature, in which, though reason is the standard, passion is the motive force" (p. 26); states that Pope's "most recurrent theme is satire itself, its necessity, its nature, its nobility" (p. 29); and concludes that "Pope's receit for satire is built upon his view of the genre as at once sanctified and secular, poetic and plain spoken" (p. 32).

259. Adler, Jacob H. "Pope and the Rules of Prosody," *PMLA*, LXXVI (1961), 218–26.

Examines Pope's "own stated rules" on prosody; compares "Pope's views with the general critical opinion of the century . . ." (p. 218); studies Pope's actual practice in comparison with his rules; and concludes that, although there is some agreement, Pope "greatly . . . ignored most of his 'rules' in his own work" (p. 219).

260. ———. *The Reach of Art: A Study in the Prosody of Pope.* University of Florida Monographs—Humanities, no. 16. Gainesville: University of Florida Press, 1964.

Provides a detailed analysis of Pope's "prosodic technique as the eighteenth century understood it" (p. 8). Adler studies the variety of Pope's rhetorical devices, meter, diction, and sound in each of the major poems.

Reviewed by Arthur W. Hoffman, *JEGP*, LXIV (1965), 738–40.

261. Allen, Robert J. "Pope and the Sister Arts," *Pope and His Contemporaries: Essays Presented to George Sher-*

burn. Edited by James L. Clifford and Louis A. Landa. Oxford: Clarendon Press, 1949.

Focuses on painting as a source for Pope's poetic imagery and discusses Pope's relationship with Charles Jervas and Pope's awareness of the tradition of comparing the painter and the poet. See also 186.

262. *Awad, Louis. "Pope and Poetic Diction," *Studies in Literature.* Cairo, Egypt: The Anglo-Egyptian Bookshop, 1954.

263. Bagnani, Gilbert. "The Classical Technique: Virgil, Dante and Pope," *Phoenix,* II (1947), 2–14.

In considering the verbal lucidity of Pope's couplets, Bagnani suggests that "we fail to appreciate the accuracy and the truth of many of Pope's scenes because the accuracy and precision of his vocabulary fails to evoke in us an immediate response" (p. 13).

264. Balliet, Conrad A. "The History and Rhetoric of the Triplet," *PMLA,* LXXX (1965), 528–34.

In describing the history of the English use of the triplet (primarily by Dryden), Balliet finds that although Pope objected to the employment of the triplet, he utilized it seventy-five times in some 3,000 lines of his poetry.

265. Bateson, F. W. "Pun and Metaphor and Pope," *EIC,* IX (1959), 437–39.

Bateson disagrees with Max Bluestone's (see 269) and Aubrey L. Williams' (see 313) interpretation of a pun in lines 318–19 of *Essay on Criticism* on the basis that an "ignorance of Latin" has caused both critics to misinterpret the couplet. Bateson concludes with an attack on Maynard Mack (see 295), maintaining that "Pope *always* stressed heterogeneity" (p. 439) in his use of antithesis. See also 287.

266. Berry, Francis. *Poets' Grammar: Person, Time and Mood in Poetry.* London: Routledge & Kegan Paul, 1958.

Chapter six, part II, "Pope and the Verb Simple," contains a brief analysis of Pope's use of the indicative mood and the "single tense" of verbs.

Reviewed in *TLS,* May 16, 1958, p. 270.

267. Bishop, Carter R. "General Themes in Pope's Satires," *West Virginia University Bulletin: Philological Papers,* VI (1949), 54–68.

Provides a discussion of Pope's technique of satirical attacks on such themes as literary patronage, the indigent and mediocre poet, decadent drama and the opera, virtuosi, educators and schools, the moneyed classes, and politics. Bishop concludes that Pope's satires were not restricted to personalities, but included current and universal topics of interest.

268. Bluestone, Max. "Pun and Metaphor and Pope," *EIC,* IX (1959), 440–43.

Defends his interpretation (see 269) of Pope's use of the "suppressed" metaphor against Aubrey L. Williams' attack (see 313).

269. ———. "The Suppressed Metaphor in Pope," *EIC,* VIII (1958), 347–54.

Examines the inactive metaphor in *Essay on Criticism,* II, 305-36; discusses the function of the "exemplary figures" in the passage; and comments on "inconsistency" of the suppressed metaphor in Pope's *Epilogue to the Satires,* dialogue II. Bluestone also considers the development of Pope's extended metaphor in regard to Cibber and Theobald (*Dunciad,* I, 118–26). See also 265, 268, and 313.

270. Boyce, Benjamin. *The Character-Sketches in Pope's Poems.* Durham, N.C.: Duke University Press, 1962.

Focuses on "the art and the craft" and the literary tradition of Pope's character-sketches rather than the portraiture of individuals, examines Pope's method and revision of character-sketches in successive drafts or editions, and investigates Pope's theory of the ruling passion. See also 176.

Reviewed by Curt A. Zimansky, *PQ,* XLII (1963), 366–67; *TLS,* September 14, 1962, p. 690.

271. Bredenberg, Henrik N., Jr. "Pope's Early Poetry: A Study of Imagery and Metaphor." Unpublished Ph.D. dis-

sertation, Florida State University, 1967, *DA*, XXVIII (1967), 1781.

Contains a detailed examination of imagery and metaphor in the *Pastorals, Messiah, Windsor Forest, Essay on Criticism, Rape of the Lock,* and *Eloisa to Abelard.*

272. Brower, Reuben Arthur. *Alexander Pope: The Poetry of Allusion.* Oxford: Clarendon Press, 1959.

Describes how Pope utilized allusions to many traditions (particularly Homer and the Roman poets); explains the main direction of Pope's development "from pastoral and georgic to the heroic and the Horatian" (p. viii); and studies the "poetic character and design" (p. vii) of Pope's poetry. Brower examines Pope's use of such sources as Homer, Horace, Ovid, Virgil, Theocritus, Spenser, Milton, Dryden, Boileau, Corneille, and Racine. See also 174 and 176.

Reviewed by F. W. Bateson, *Spectator,* November 13, 1959, p. 676; *TLS,* December 25, 1959, p. 756; Donald F. Bond, *MP,* LVIII (1960), 132–34; Patrick Cruttwell, *HudR,* XIII (1960), 438–41; H. V. D. Dyson, *RES,* n.s., XI (1960), 432–34; Jacques Golliet, *EA,* XIII (1960), 378–79; Ralph M. Williams, *CE,* XXII (1960), 57; Hoyt Trowbridge, *PQ,* XL (1961), 414–16; Robert W. Rogers, *JEGP,* LX (1961), 591–92; Aubrey L. Williams, *MLN,* LXXVI (1961), 359–65.

273. Brown, Wallace Cable. *The Triumph of Form: A Study of the Later Masters of the Heroic Couplet.* Chapel Hill: University of North Carolina Press, 1948.

In chapter one, Brown traces the technical and esthetic development of the heroic couplet and discusses Pope's contribution to this tradition with excerpts from the *Pastorals, Windsor Forest, Essay on Man, Moral Essays,* and *Epistle to Dr. Arbuthnot.* In chapter two, Brown studies Pope's influence on John Gay.

274. Bullitt, John, and Bate, W. Jackson. "Distinctions Between Fancy and Imagination in Eighteenth-Century English Criticism," *MLN,* LX (1945), 8–15.

Contains a discussion of the various distinctions made between the two terms before, and by Coleridge and Wordsworth. A brief reference to Mrs. Piozzi's *British Synonymy* (1794) provides her definition of *Rape of the Lock* as an example of fancy.

275. Chatman, Seymour. "Comparing Metrical Styles," *Style in Language*. Edited by Thomas A. Sebeok. New York: Technology Press of Massachusetts Institute of Technology and John Wiley & Sons, 1960.

> Describes and contrasts the metrical structures of Donne's *Satire II* and *Satire IV* with Pope's imitation of both satires, analyzes the segmental phonological effects of both styles, and concludes with a brief survey of recent criticism relevant to the metrical styles of both poets.

> Reviewed by Thomas J. Roberts, *WHR*, xvi (1962), 285–86.

276. Dixon, Peter. "'Talking upon Paper': Pope and Eighteenth Century Conversation," *ES*, xlvi (1965), 36–44.

> Examines Pope's method of relating "poetry to contemporary speech-habits" (p. 36) and studies Pope's *delicacy* in his conversational raillery.

277. Eckhoff, Lorentz. "Stoicism in Shakespeare . . . and Elsewhere," *Studies in English Language and Literature Presented to Dr. Karl Brunner on the Occasion of His Seventieth Birthday*. Edited by Siegfried Korninger. Vienna: Braümuller, 1957.

> Contains a brief discussion of Pope's ethics in terms of the poet's stoical portrait-types.

278. Edwards, Thomas Robert, Jr. "The Colors of Fancy: An Image Cluster in Pope," *MLN*, lxxiii (1958), 485–89.

> States that a "cluster of images" which appeared in Pope's letter to Henry Cromwell (1711) was echoed in Pope's poetry, and briefly cites examples of this image clustèr in the *Pastorals, Temple of Fame, Essay on Man, Moral Essays, Rape of the Lock,* and *Dunciad*.

279. Forseth, Roger Daniels. "The Function of Imagery in the Lyric: Pope to Wordsworth." Unpublished Ph.D. dissertation, Northwestern University, 1956, *DA*, xvii (1957), 852–53.

> Observes the "precise changes in poetic technique" (p. 852) from the Augustans to the Romanticists and concludes that poetic diction as employed by such poets as Pope "is

for the most part highly functional" and that the complex
organization and function of early Augustan imagery is
found in the lyrics of subsequent poets.

280. Fussell, Paul. *The Rhetorical World of Augustan Humanism: Ethics and Imagery from Swift to Burke.* Oxford:
Clarendon Press, 1965.

Contains sections on Pope and his poetry. Fussell states
that this work "is about both the ethical convictions and the
related rhetorical techniques—especially the polemic imagery
—" of Pope and five other eighteenth-century writers "who,
because they exhibit a marvellous concurrence of imagination, design, and method, can be said to postulate a self-
contained rhetorical world" (p. vii).

281. Göller, Karl Heinz. "Die *Poetic Diction* des 18. Jahrhun-
derts," *Deutsche Vierteljahresschrift für Literaturwissen-
schaft und Geistesgeschichte,* XXXVIII (March, 1964), 24–39.

Examines Pope's style in relationship to the eighteenth-
century concept of poetic diction.

282. Greene, Donald J. "Dramatic Texture in Pope," *From
Sensibility to Romanticism: Essays Presented to Frederick
A. Pottle.* Edited by Frederick W. Hilles and Harold Bloom.
New York: Oxford University Press, 1965.

Discusses the dramatic structure of *Imitation of the
Second Satire of the Second Book, Epistle to Arbuthnot,* and
First Satire of the Second Book. Greene states that "the
poems in which Pope most strikingly creates drama by use
of a shifting series of *personae* . . . are generally his later
ones" (p. 41). See also 209.

283. Hagstrum, Jean H. *The Sister Arts: The Tradition of
Literary Pictorialism and English Poetry from Dryden to
Gray.* Chicago: University of Chicago Press, 1958.

Examines Pope's kinship to and use of classical art, especially baroque. Hagstrum cites examples from *Rape of
the Lock, Temple of Fame,* translation of the *Iliad,* and
Pope's satirical character-portraits in order to substantiate
the contention that Pope "drew the analogy between poetry
and painting" (p. 241), and that "Pope's icon . . . has all
the marks of pictoral arrangement: design, light, color, and

the grouping of subordinate figures around a central one"
(p. 218).

284. Herring, George Dewitt. "Satiric Devices and Themes in
Pope, 1728–1743." Unpublished Ph.D. dissertation, University of Wisconsin, 1953.

Provides a detailed analysis of Pope's use of the satiric
genre and utilization of the following devices: names and
persons, structure, texture, parody, diction, theme, and imitation. Herring concludes that Pope's "satiric ambiguity"
works through his use of language and satirical devices.

285. Hooker, Edward Niles. "Humour in the Age of Pope,"
HLQ, xi (1948), 361–85.

Discusses the etymology and use of the word *humour* in
the seventeenth and eighteenth centuries, and makes a passing
reference to Pope's theory of the ruling passion.

286. Hughes, Richard Edward. "The Sense of the Ridiculous:
Ridicule as a Rhetorical Device in the Poetry of Dryden
and Pope." Unpublished Ph.D. dissertation, University of
Wisconsin, 1954.

Studies the theory and practice of ridicule as a rhetorical
device in the poetry and prose of Pope and Dryden. Hughes
also traces the classical sources for a theory of ridicule
and discusses the "reaffirmation of classicism in rhetoric"
(p. 6).

287. James, G. Ingli, and Bateson, F. W. "Prose and Poetry
and Mack," *EIC,* x (1960), 114–16.

James defends Maynard Mack's (see 295) analysis of
Pope's use of figures of contrast against Bateson's criticism
(see 265). Bateson answers James by admitting that he did
"misinterpret a crucial sentence." However, Bateson maintains that Mack's argument is obscure.

288. Jernigan, Jack Julian. "Levels of Meaning in the Poetry
of Pope: A Study of His Use of Ambiguity." Unpublished
Ph.D. dissertation, Vanderbilt University, 1955, *DA,* xv
(1955), 2207.

Defines and discriminates nine types of ambiguity employed by Pope: strategic ambiguity, paronomasia, peri-
phrasis, mimicry, allusion, juxtaposition, paradox, irony,

and dramatic pose. Jernigan analyzes the function of ambiguity in *Rape of the Lock, Dunciad, Essay on Man, Epistle to a Lady,* and *Epistle to Augustus.*

289. Johnston, Elizabeth. "Freedom in Restraint," *If By Your Art: Testament to Percival Hunt.* Edited by Agnes Lynch Starrett. Pittsburgh: University of Pittsburgh Press, 1948.

Discusses the various techniques Pope employed in order to achieve variety within the confines of the heroic couplet.

290. *Jones, John A. "Line Structure and Sentence Form in Pope's Couplet." Unpublished Ph.D. dissertation, University of Florida, 1961.

291. Kernan, Alvin B. *The Plot of Satire.* New Haven: Yale University Press, 1965.

Emphasizes Pope's satirical method in the following chapters: "The Rhetoric of Satire: *Peri Bathous*" and "Everything and Nothing: *The Dunciad.*" Kernan also comments *passim* on *Epilogue to the Satires, Epistle to Dr. Arbuthnot, Essay on Man,* and *Imitations of Horace.*

Reviewed by Philip Pinkus, *PQ,* XLV (1966), 518-20.

292. Leavis, F. R. "Pope," *Essential Articles for the Study of Alexander Pope.* Edited by Maynard Mack. Hamden, Conn.: Shoestring Press, 1964.

Employing various passages from Pope's satiric poems, Leavis examines Pope's "satiric variety," the "poised and subtle variety" of his "satiric tones," and his satiric wit. Leavis also discusses Pope's relationship to the metaphysical tradition and to Dryden. Also published in Leavis, F. R. *Revaluation.* London: Chatto & Windus, 1935, pp. 68-91.

293. *Le Page, R. B. "A Rhythmical Framework for the Five Types," *English and German Studies,* VI (1957), 92-103.

294. Mack, Maynard. "The Muse of Satire," *YR,* XLI (1951), 80-92.

Examines the rhetorical nature of Pope's satires and the three voices of Pope's speaker or persona. Mack emphasizes the importance of distinguishing between Pope as a man and as a poet. See also 200.

295. Mack, Maynard. " 'Wit and Poetry and Pope': Some Observations on His Imagery," *Pope and His Contemporaries: Essays Presented to George Sherburn*. Edited by James L. Clifford and Louis A. Landa. Oxford: Clarendon Press, 1949.

Comments on the definition of Pope's poetry as "a poetry of statement" by discussing how Pope's metaphorical effects "do not disturb a logical surface of statement" (p. 22). Mack analyzes Pope's use of metaphor, allusion, pun, juxtaposition, and portrait-sketches. See also 185, 186, 265, and 287.

296. Parkin, Rebecca Price. "Alexander Pope's Use of the Implied Dramatic Speaker," *CE*, XI (1949), 137–41.

Examines the significance and the function of the implied dramatic speaker in the *Pastorals, Eloisa to Abelard, Rape of the Lock, Essay on Man, Essay on Criticism*, and *Dunciad*.

297. ———. *The Poetic Workmanship of Alexander Pope*. Minneapolis: University of Minnesota Press, 1955; reprint, New York: Octagon Books, 1966.

Explicating key passages from Pope's poetry, Parkin studies Pope's employment of the implied dramatic speaker, irony, humor, parallelism, antithesis, paradox, metaphor, tension, tonal variation, narrative elements, genre, imitation, and the theme of "correctible evil."

Reviewed by Curt A. Zimansky, *PQ*, XXXV (1956), 320; Robert W. Rogers, *CE*, XVII (1955), 421–22; Robert M. Schmitz, *JEGP*, LV (1956), 511–13; *TLS*, June 1, 1957, p. 330; Reuben Arthur Brower, *MLN*, LXXII (1957), 222–25; Jacques Golliet, *EA*, X (1957), 258–59; Margaret M. Blum, *SWR*, XLI (1956), 206–7.

298. ———. "The Quality of Alexander Pope's Humor," *CE*, XIV (1953), 197–202.

Explains the didactic function of Pope's humor in *Essay on Criticism, Essay on Man, Rape of the Lock*, Dialogue I of *Epilogue to the Satires*, and *Dunciad*. Parkin states that Pope's humor helps to establish the following qualities in his poetry: "clearness, balance of viewpoint, and universal appeal" (p. 197).

299. Patten, Faith Harris. "The Nature of Figurative Language in the Poetry of Pope." Unpublished Ph.D. dissertation, Rutgers—The State University, 1967, *DA*, XXVIII (1967), 2258.

> Finds that "Pope's figurative language is rhetorical: . . . it is designed to persuade the reader to accept the opinion, attitude, or idea embodied by the poem," and that a figure "may decorate the verse, illustrate the argument, or evaluate a character or an idea."

300. St. Vincent, Edwin Harold. "Aspects of Pope's Imagery." Unpublished Ph.D. dissertation, Columbia University, 1962, *DA*, XXIV (1963), 286.

> Analyzes seven categories of both descriptive and figurative imagery found in Pope's poetry: nature, animals, physical phenomena, people, the body, the imagination, and the arts; describes "the development of Pope's style in relation to his imagery"; and ascertains that movement or motion, perpetually present in Pope's poetry, is aesthetically and morally significant.

301. Sherburn, George. "Pope at Work," *Essays on the Eighteenth Century Presented to David Nichol Smith in Honour of His Seventieth Birthday*. Oxford: Clarendon Press, 1945.

> Discusses the significance of Pope's habit of working "on several poems at once" (p. 51), but concentrates on a detailed analysis (citing examples from the manuscripts of *Essay on Man*) of the four procedures Pope seemed to follow in the composition of his poetry: making initial prose notes, turning the prose into verse paragraphs, shifting and arranging the notes and paragraphs into an effective structure, and perfecting the couplets.

> Reviewed by Maynard Mack, *PQ*, XXV (1946), 158–61.

302. Siegrist, Ottmar K. "Arcade: An Antedating," *N&Q*, CCV (1960), 33.

> Suggests that "the earliest occurrence of sense two of *arcade*" is found in a letter from Pope to Edward Blount dated June 2, 1725, rather than the 1731 listing given by the *OED*.

303. Stanley, E. G. "Dr. Johnson's Use of the Word *Also*," *N&Q*, CCIX (1964), 298–99.

States that both Pope and Johnson avoided use of the word *also*.

304. Sypher, Wylie. "Arabesque in Verse (Reconsiderations III)," *KR*, VII (1945), 456–66.

Examines the close parallels between "the complexity of the rococo-arabesque design" (p. 459) and the "surface" or external transitions of Pope's verse.

305. ————. *Rococo to Cubism in Art and Literature*. New York: Random House, 1960.

In the chapter entitled "Pope and the Rococo Situation," Sypher states that Pope's style, known as rococo because he created poetry as ideas and ornaments, initiated "a counter-movement against baroque and late-baroque in verse" (p. 10).

306. Tillotson, Geoffrey. *Augustan Studies*. London: Athlone Press, 1961.

Major emphasis is placed on a detailed analysis of Pope's poetic diction in satire, epic, pastoral, georgic, and descriptions and on his use of the heroic couplet. Tillotson also explicates Pope's *Epistle to Harley*, discusses the *Minor Poems*, and comments on the poet's letters as found in Sherburn's edition (see 670).

307. ————. "Eighteenth-Century Poetic Diction," *Eighteenth-Century English Literature: Modern Essays in Criticism*. Edited by James L. Clifford. New York: Oxford University Press, 1959.

Discusses the reasons why eighteenth-century poets used the kind of vocabulary they did, analyzes the various types and purposes of the diction employed, and contrasts the poetic diction of the nineteenth and eighteenth centuries. See also 185.

308. ————. "The Methods of Description in Eighteenth- and Nineteenth-Century Poetry," *Restoration and Eighteenth-Century Literature. Essays in Honor of Alan Dugald Mc-*

Killop. Edited by Carroll Camden. Chicago: University of Chicago Press for William Marsh Rice University, 1963.

Quotes a passage from *Windsor Forest* and one from *Eloisa to Abelard* as examples of Pope's use of syntax for descriptive purposes and states that "in none of his poems does Pope allow the syntax of the normal couplet to interfere with the building up of the paragraph . . ." (p. 237). See also 182.

309. Tillotson, Geoffrey. *On the Poetry of Pope.* 2d ed. Oxford: Clarendon Press, 1950.

Focuses on the connotation of correctness in the context of Pope's attitude toward nature and of the three distinct *tours* in poetry: design, language, and versification. Tillotson also examines the variety and complexity of Pope's syntax and diction.

310. ———. "Pope and the Common Reader," *SR*, LXVI (1958), 44–78.

Provides an extensive analysis of Pope's diction, especially in *Essay on Man.* Tillotson studies Pope's syntax, versification, and imagery and reveals "how Pope's wish to reach the common reader . . . affected the choice of his medium and the art with which he used it" (p. 44).

311. Weinbrot, Howard D. "The Pattern of Formal Verse Satire in the Restoration and the Eighteenth Century," *PMLA*, LXXX (1965), 394–401.

Describes Popes adherence to the requirement that the formal verse satire "praise the virtue opposed to the vice attacked" (p. 396). Weinbrot concludes that Pope's use of the "pattern of praise and blame" substantiates Pope's adherence "to the concept of formal verse satire described by Dryden" (p. 394).

312. Williams, Aubrey L. "Alexander Pope's 'Knack' at Versifying," *All These to Teach: Essays in Honor of C. A. Robertson.* Edited by Robert A. Bryan, Alton C. Morris, A. A. Murphree, and Aubrey L. Williams. Gainesville: University of Florida Press, 1965.

Traces Pope's use of the word *knack* in order "to illustrate the ironic and self-conscious ways in which he could seem to depreciate his own long labors" (p. 173). Williams explicates *Moral Essay*, II, 231–42, and *Second Satire of the Second Book*, 69–72, as examples of Pope's hard work, not luck or knack at versifying.

313. Williams, Aubrey L. "Submerged Metaphor in Pope," *EIC*, IX (1959), 197–201.

Attacks Max Bluestone's discussion (see 269) of Pope's imagery. Williams maintains that the dress metaphor in lines 305–36 of *Essay on Criticism* "is not suppressed and it never becomes otiose" (p. 198). See also 265 and 268.

314. Williams, Charles. *The Image of the City and Other Essays*. London: Oxford University Press, 1958.

Contains a brief statement concerning Pope's heroic couplet as the image of "Good Sense."

315. Wimsatt, William Kurtz, Jr. *The Verbal Icon*. Lexington: University of Kentucky Press, 1954.

In a chapter entitled "One Relation of Rhyme to Reason," Wimsatt compares Pope's rhymes with those of Chaucer; and in a second chapter, "Rhetoric and Poems: Alexander Pope," he describes "five main types of relation between theory and poems" (p. 169) and discusses Pope's theory on the basis of his (Wimsatt's) five categories. The latter chapter is reprinted from *English Institute Essays*, 1948, edited by D. A. Robertson, Jr. See also 172 and 219.

PASTORALS AND WINDSOR FOREST

316. Congleton, James Edmund. *Theories of Pastoral Poetry in England, 1684–1798*. Gainesville: University of Florida Press, 1952.

> Contains references to Pope as the chief exponent of the neoclassical theory of pastoral poetry; cites Pope's defense of this theory against Ambrose Philips; and explains Pope's doctrine in his "Discourse on Pastoral Poetry" and *Guardian*, no. 40.

317. Hauser, David R. "Pope's Lodona and the Uses of Mythology," *SEL*, VI (1966), 465–82.

> Explores Pope's use of traditional myth, such as the metamorphosis of Lodona for the following purposes: "It serves as the third and climactic hunt episode," "introduces the metaphor of reflection, provides the transition from the world of the Forest to the world at large," and represents "allegorically the entire course of the war and the anticipated effect of the Peace which will extend the influence of Anne throughout the world" (p. 466).

318. Hilty, Peter Daniel. "English Pastoral Poetry from Pope to Wordsworth." Unpublished Ph.D. dissertation, University of Missouri, 1958, *DA*, XIX (1958), 317–18.

> Classifies pastoral literature into five groups, surveys pastorals from Pope to Wordsworth, and concludes that Romantic poetry did not develop directly from the pastoral of the eighteenth century, because "the Romantic attitude demanded intellectual compromises which the neoclassical pastoralist, intent upon teaching a lesson, could never make" (p. 318).

319. *Jurgens, Heather. " 'Windsor Forest' and Augustan Stability," *Unisa English Studies*, XI (1967), 15–22.

320. Kiehl, James M. "Windsor-Forest as Epical Counterpart," *Thoth*, vol. VII, no. 2 (1966), pp. 53–67.

> States that the poem corresponds to the traditional epic in "tone, imagery, structure, and theme" and that "the

peace it celebrates anticipates a universality integrally related to the traditional epic" (p. 53).

321. Mack, Maynard. "On Reading Pope," *CE*, VII (1946), 263–73.

Originally delivered as an address at Columbia University in 1944 and reprinted in *CE*, XXII (1960), 99–107. Mack discusses the reasons why Pope's critics have not given his verse close scrutiny and explicates passages from *Windsor Forest, Essay on Man,* and *Epistle to Bathurst,* focusing on the subtlety of Pope's organization.

322. Maxwell, J. C. "Pope's 'Spring' and Milton's 'In Adventum Veris,' " *N&Q*, CCXI (1966), 212.

Notes that lines 57–58 of Pope's "Spring" are recalled by Milton's imitation of the Virgilian lines in his *Fifth Elegy,* 129–30.

323. Melchiori, Giorgio. "Pope in Arcady: The Theme of *Et in Arcadia Ego* in His *Pastorals,*" *English Miscellany*, XIV (1963), 83–93.

Indicates that Pope's closest model for his *Pastorals* was a painting by Poussin and describes similar themes on the "realization of the presence of death . . ." in Poussin's works and in the poetry of Pope.

324. Moore, John Robert. "*Windsor Forest* and William III," *MLN*, LXVI (1951), 451–54.

Maintains that "the implicit attack on William III . . . was certainly partisan in tone" (p. 451) and that the entire poem reflects a Tory (or anti-Williamite) bias. See also 219.

325. Nierenberg, Edwin H. "Two Essayists on Man: Alexander Pope and E. M. Forster." Unpublished Ph.D. dissertation, University of Pittsburgh, 1962, *DA*, XXIII (1963), 4678.

Compares Pope and Forster on the basis of their similar views on the nature of man, life, art, religion, passion, reason, and God in *Windsor Forest* and *A Passage to India.*

326. O'Hehir, Brendan P. "Vergil's First *Georgic* and Denham's *Cooper's Hill*," *PQ*, XLII (1963), 542–47.

States that Pope's echo of the first line of "Spring" and the last line of *Windsor Forest* is an imitation of Virgil; but more significantly the echo labels *Windsor Forest* as Pope's effort to produce a georgic.

327. Oliver, Leslie M. "New Sources for Pope's Eclogues?" *Research Studies of the State College of Washington*, XV (1947), 109–12.

Suggests that Cowley's poem "The Spring," and especially the Elizabethan play *Mucedorus* (IV, iii, 24–55), are possible sources for lines 73–76 of Pope's eclogue "Summer" in *Windsor Forest*.

328. Provost, Foster. "Pope's Pastorals: An Exercise in Poetical Technique," *Contributions to the Humanities, 1954*. Louisiana State University Studies: Humanities Series, no. 5. Baton Rouge: Louisiana State University Press, 1954.

Compares Pope's eclogue "Spring" with Dryden's translation of Virgil's *Third Pastoral* and examines the extent to which Pope observed René Rapin's rules for writing pastorals. Provost also studies Pope's experimentation with poetical technique and concludes that the rules applied in the *Pastorals* form the basis for the section on versification in *Essay on Criticism*.

329. *Schlüter, Kurt. "Popes *Windsor Forest*, Ein Ortsgedicht in Pastoraler Gestaltung," *Anglia*, LXXIX (1961), 177–203.

330. Schmitz, Robert M. (ed.). *Pope's Windsor Forest, 1712: A Study of the Washington University Holograph*. Washington University Studies, n.s., Language and Literature, no. 21. St. Louis: Washington University Press, 1952.

Prints the text of the 1712 manuscript of *Windsor Forest*, investigates the historical background of the text, and systematically analyzes "the several hundred" alterations as a basis for studying "Pope's early poetical development" (p. 4).

Reviewed by William Kurtz Wimsatt, Jr., *PQ*, XXXII (1953), 284–86; F. W. Baxter, *MLR*, XLIX (1954), 230–31; John Butt, *JEGP*, LIII (1954), 123–25; Arthur Friedman, *MP*, LI (1953), 281; Harold Williams, *RES*, n.s., V (1954), 195–97.

331. Warren, Austin. *Rage for Order: Essays in Criticism.* Chicago: University of Chicago Press, 1948.

Chapter three (which first appeared as "The Mask of Pope," *SR*, LIV [1946], 19–33) deals with the discrepancy between the theory of Augustan poetry and neoclassical poetry. Warren discusses Pope's development "from the elegantly decorative to the richly—even the grotesquely—expressive" (p. 41) and analyzes the *Pastorals, Rape of the Lock,* and *Dunciad.*

332. Wasserman, Earl R. *The Subtler Language: Critical Readings of Neoclassic and Romantic Poems.* Baltimore: Johns Hopkins Press, 1959.

Chapter four contains a detailed explication of *Windsor Forest* as a political poem pervaded by the theme of *concordia discors.* Wasserman compares Denham's *Cooper's Hill* with *Windsor Forest* and interprets the symbolism in the latter poem.

333. Aden, John M. "The Doctrinal Design of *An Essay on Criticism*," *CE*, XXII (1961), 311–15.

> Examines part I of the essay, focusing on Pope's theory of nature, wit, judgment, and art in relationship to the "ancients" and to the "rules."

334. ———. " 'First Follow Nature': Strategy and Stratification in *An Essay on Criticism*," *JEGP*, LV (1956), 604–17.

> Provides a detailed explication of Pope's essay which takes into consideration Pope's theory of art and concept of nature and his use of structural design, rhetorical pattern, versification, grammar, ambiguity, and allusion.

335. Adler, Jacob H. "Balance in Pope's *Essays*," *ES*, XLIII (1962), 457–67.

> Studies the method, cause, and effect of balance in *Essay on Criticism* and *Essay on Man*. Adler also examines the relationship of balance to other rhetorical and prosodic techniques within both poems.

336. Cameron, J. M. "Mr. Tillotson and Mr. Pope," *Dublin Review*, CCXXXIII (1959), 153–70.

> Finds that academic specialization in America has led to a serious neglect of the study of the "history of ideas" in literature. To illustrate his contention, Cameron examines Geoffrey Tillotson's treatment (see 248) of Pope's concept of nature in *Essay on Criticism*. In order to clarify Pope's concept, Cameron explicates part I of the essay and describes how "Pope *uses* the ambiguities of the concept" (p. 158).
>
> Reviewed by Aubrey L. Williams, *PQ*, XXXIX (1960), 346–47.

337. De Lisle, Harold F. "Structure in Part I of Pope's *Essay on Criticism*," *ELN*, I (1963), 14–17.

> States that in order for Pope to defend his classical thesis (a good critic is one who adheres to ancient rules), Pope structured part I "in accordance with the traditional divi-

sions of classical oration which is appropriate to argumentation" (p. 14).

338. Empson, William. *The Structure of Complex Words*. London: Chatto & Windus, 1951.

Chapter three (reprinted from "Wit in the *Essay on Criticism*," *HudR*, II [1950], 559–77) contains an analysis of Pope's use of the term *wit* in *Essay on Criticism*. Empson also examines the various levels of meaning of the term. See also 219.

339. Fenner, Arthur, Jr. "The Unity of Pope's *Essay on Criticism*," *PQ*, XXXIX (1960), 435–46.

Provides a detailed analysis of the structural unity within the couplets, and the internal, transitional, and sequential unity of the verse paragraphs and the three larger sections. Fenner also explains how Pope achieves these levels of unity and examines the essay's theme in relationship to the poem's structural organization. See also 219.

340. Fogle, Richard Harter. "Metaphors of Organic Unity in Pope's *Essay on Criticism*," *Tulane Studies in English*, XIII (1963), 51–58.

Quotes part I, 68–79; part II, 243–52 and 484–93; and states that "all three figures—from the human body, from architecture, and from painting—suggest the inseparable relationships and indivisible unity . . . between the neoclassical critical theory of Pope and the Romantic organicism of Coleridge" (p. 53).

341. Hamm, Victor M. "Pope and Malebranche: A Note on the *Essay on Criticism*: Part II," *PQ*, XXIV (1945), 65–70.

Finds parallels between Nicolas Malebranche and Pope and suggests that part II of Pope's essay reflects "the spirit and method" of part II, book II, of Malebranche's *De la recherche de la vérité*.

342. Hooker, Edward Niles. "Pope on Wit: The *Essay on Criticism*," *Eighteenth-Century English Literature: Modern Essays in Criticism*. Edited by James L. Clifford. New York: Oxford University Press, 1959.

Explicates the essay by defining Pope's concept of *wit,* by discussing the contemporary controversies and thought available to Pope while composing the essay, and by suggesting the direction of Pope's thinking in the poem. See also 185, 215, and 219.

343. Jones, H. W. "Some Further Pope-Dryden Indebtedness?" *N&Q,* CXCVIII (1953), 199–200.

States that lines 346–47 of *Essay on Criticism* suggest Dryden, while lines 21–28 seem to echo Wycherley's *The Plain Dealer.* Jones also notes Pope's possible debt to Dryden for lines 203 and 325 of *Epistle to Dr. Arbuthnot.*

344. *Kallich, Martin. "Image and Theme in Pope's *Essay on Criticism,*" *Ball State University Forum,* vol. VIII, no. 3 (1967), pp. 54–60.

345. ———. "Pegasus on the Seesaw: Balance and Antithesis in Pope's *Essay on Criticism,*" *TSL,* XII (1967), 57–68.

Studies in detail Pope's employment of the "rhetorical figure of antithesis" and concludes that the "approximately sixty oscillating antitheses reinforce Pope's didactic intention . . . structure the total work . . . and express the theme" of the poem.

346. Klinger, Samuel. "Whig Aesthetics," *ELH,* XVI (1949), 135–50.

Contains a brief reference to *Essay on Criticism,* III, 711–14. Kliger states that the passage reveals Pope's opposition to neoclassic rules and reflects "Pope's scorn of rule-ridden France . . ." (p. 145).

347. Mace, Dean Tolle. "The Doctrine of Sound and Sense in Augustan Poetic Theory," *RES,* n.s., II (1951), 129–39.

Examines the Augustan theory of sound and sense, or "the problem of relating non-meaning to meaning" (p. 130), especially as the theory is expounded in *Essay on Criticism* and Preface to *Iliad.*

348. *Means, James A. "One Aspect of Balance in Pope's *Essay on Criticism,*" *AN&Q,* V (1967), 68–69.

349. Monk, Samuel Holt. "A Grace Beyond the Reach of Art," *Essential Articles for the Study of Alexander Pope.* Edited by Maynard Mack. Hamden, Conn.: Shoestring Press, 1964.

> Cites *Essay on Criticism* (I, 141–45, 152–57); provides a detailed analysis of the genealogy of the word *grace* by comparing its employment by Pope to passages from the works of Roger de Piles, the elder Pliny, Cicero, Quintilian, Cesare Ripa, Castiglione, Dolce, Vasari, Lomazzo, Franciscus Junius, and Rapin; and substantiates the fact that Pope's "use of the word *grace* and his interpretation of its meaning" were "well established in English criticism" (p. 51) and were an expression of "traditional critical ideas in traditional language" (p. 53). Also published in *Journal of the History of Ideas,* V (1944), 131–50.

350. Morse, J. Mitchell. "Pope's 'Words are like Leaves,'" *N&Q,* CCI (1956), 430–31.

> Cites medieval churchmen—Abelard, Richard of Saint Victor, and Gregory the Great—as three possible sources for *Essay on Criticism,* II, 205–10.

351. Pettit, Henry. "Opposite Metaphor in Pope's *Essay on Criticism,*" *BA,* XXXV (1961), 225–30.

> Examines the watch, light, and the prism-glass images in part II of *Essay on Criticism.* Pettit suggests that the poem's metaphors relate to either "imagery of nature, imagery of fallibility, or imagery of aspiration" (p. 229).

352. *Ramsey, Paul. "The Watch of Judgment: Relativism and *An Essay on Criticism,*" *Studies in Criticism and Aesthetics, 1660–1800: Essays in Honor of Samuel Holt Monk.* Edited by Howard Anderson and John S. Shea. Minneapolis: University of Minnesota Press, 1967.

353. Riggs, E. S. "A Little Learning," *AN&Q,* III (1965), 135.

> Suggests that line 130 of Drayton's *Of Poets and Poesie* may be a possible source for Pope's *Essay on Criticism,* I, 215.

354. Sanders, Charles. "Toward a Definition of Nature in Pope's *Essay on Criticism.*" Unpublished Ph.D. disserta-

tion, University of Michigan, 1965, *DA,* xxvi (1966), 2728–29.

Accepts "Lovejoy's theory of *uniformitarianism* and its currency in Neoclassical aesthetics, [in order] to learn how it may be said to influence the literary idealization of Nature and promote any grounds for ambiguity in the *consensus gentium* to which Pope's *Essay* was heir."

355. Schmitz, Robert M. *Pope's Essay on Criticism, 1709. A Study of the Bodleian Manuscript Text with Facsimiles, Transcripts, and Variants.* St. Louis: Washington University Press, 1962.

Contains a holograph copy of *Essay on Criticism.* The transcript is accompanied by annotations, footnotes, and a discussion of each revision. A section entitled "Plagiarism and Wit" deals with Pope's footnotes to sources in the manuscript and with the poet's concept of wit.

356. Smith, A. J. M. "The Critic's Task: Frye's Latest Work," *Canadian Literature,* no. 20 (1964), pp. 6–14.

Shows a parallel in subject content of Frye's *The Well-Tempered Critic* and Pope's *Essay on Criticism.*

357. Smith, Constance I. "Hume: A Reference to Pope," *N&Q,* ccv (1960), 115.

Agrees with J. C. Maxwell (see 112), but suggests that line 679 of *Essay on Criticism* echoes Dryden's prologue to *Love Triumphant.*

358. Stein, William Bysshe. "Pope's *Essay on Criticism*: The Play of Sophia," *Bucknell Review,* xiii (1965), 75–86.

Identifies Sophia as "Heavenly Wisdom," the "feminine creative principle behind the Trinity, the archetypal form of the Virgin Mary corresponding to the Logos (Jesus Christ)." Stein contends that Sophia's "identity" is "crucial to Pope's delicate handling of pun and connotation" in the essay.

Reviewed by Aubrey L. Williams, *PQ,* xlv (1966), 579.

359. Watson, George. *The Literary Critics: A Study of English Descriptive Criticism.* New York: Barnes & Noble, 1962.

In the chapter entitled "The Augustans," Watson traces Dryden's influence on neoclassical literary criticism; briefly discusses Pope's *Essay on Criticism*; and concludes that "the *Essay* is clever, but it is the indecent, puppyish cleverness of a precocious boy . . ." (p. 63).

360. Wilkins, A. N. "Pope and 'Appius,' " *N&Q*, ccv (1960), 292–94.

Suggests that the sensitivity to criticism demonstrated by Appius in Dennis' *Appius and Virginia* is one reason for Pope's employment of Appius' rather than Dennis' name in *Essay on Criticism*, iii, 582–87.

361. Wimsatt, William Kurtz, Jr., and Brooks, Cleanth. *Literary Criticism: A Short History*. New York: Alfred A. Knopf, 1957.

The chapter entitled "Rhetoric and Neo-Classic Wit" contains an analysis of *Essay on Criticism*. Pope's concept of nature, wit, and literary theory and his use of verbal rhetoric are explained. The authors also provide a brief statement about the "rhetorico-metaphysical tradition" (p. 247) of the fourth book of the *Dunciad*.

RAPE OF THE LOCK

362. Aden, John M. "Hero and Belinda," *N&Q,* CCII (1957), 12–13.

Finds close parallels between Marlowe's *Hero and Leander* and *Rape of the Lock.* Aden suggests that Marlowe's heroine served as a source for Pope's.

363. Avery, Emmett L. "A Poem on Dorset Garden Theatre," *Theatre Notebook,* XVIII (1964), 121–24.

Reprints a 1706 anonymous poem containing a passage which "foreshadows the passage in Pope's *Rape of the Lock* in which Belinda prepares herself at the toilet table" (p. 122).

364. Baker, Donald C. "Pope Echoes Addison?" *N&Q,* CCI (1956), 339.

Suggests line 12 of Addison's poem "To Mr. Dryden" as a possible source for *Rape of the Lock,* I, 148.

365. Bayley, John. "Twickenham and Hampstead," *National and English Review,* CXXXIV (1950), 73–76.

Briefly compares Pope's *Rape of the Lock* with Keats' *Eve of St. Agnes* and comments on Pope's portrayal of nature in *Windsor Forest.*

366. Boyce, Benjamin. "Pope, Gildon, and Salamanders," *N&Q,* CXCIV (1949), 14.

Reflects on the possibility that Pope may have read and employed letter VI of the second volume of Charles Gildon's *Post-boy Rob'd of his Mail* ("An Answer to a Letter, concerning Cabalistical opinion of Zilphs, and Salamanders") for the "machinery" in *Rape of the Lock.*

367. Brooks, Cleanth. "The Case of Miss Arabella Fermor," *The Well Wrought Urn: Studies in the Structure of Poetry.* New York: Reynal & Hitchcock, 1947.

Explicates *Rape of the Lock,* focusing on Pope's attitude toward Belinda, the "rape," and chastity. Brooks also examines the function of the sylphs, studies the imagery and symbolism in the poem, and notes parallels between *Rape of the Lock* and Milton's *Paradise Lost*. See also 219.

368. Brophy, Brigid. *Mozart the Dramatist*. New York: Harcourt, Brace, and World, 1964.

Besides a general study of eighteenth-century culture, Brophy's work includes a brief interpretation of *Rape of the Lock*.

369. *Brown, Jack R. "It's All in the Cards: Pope's Game of Ombre in *The Rape of the Lock*," *West Virginia Association of College English Teachers News Bulletin*, I (1955), 16–21.

370. Brückmann, Patricia Laureen. "Fancy's Maze: A Study of the Early Poetry of Alexander Pope." Unpublished Ph.D. dissertation, University of Toronto, 1961.

Provides an extensive analysis of Pope's *Discourse on Pastoral Poetry, Pastorals, Windsor Forest, Essay on Criticism*, and, especially, *Rape of the Lock*. Brückmann maintains that Pope's humanism is revealed in his early poems through his development of form.

371. ———. "Pope's Shock and the Count of Gabalis," *ELN*, I (1964), 261–62.

In substantiating Ariel's guardianship of Belinda's lapdog Shock, Brückmann cites Pope's source, Villars' *Le Comte de Gabalis*, which identifies dogs as transformed sylphs. Consequently, Ariel is taking care of his own kind when he guards the dog rather than the lock.

372. Carnochan, W. B. "Pope's *The Rape of the Lock*," *Explicator*, XXII (1964), item 45.

Mentions that the theme of ephemeral earthly beauty and the imperishability of art is supported by the poem's focus on one day and the imagery of the progression from light to dark.

373. Cook, Richard I. "Garth's *Dispensary* and Pope's *Rape of the Lock*," *CLAJ*, VI (1962), 107–16.

Studies the basic differences between Pope's and Garth's attitudes toward their subject matter, purpose in writing, presentation of character-types, and satirical techniques. Cook concludes that the two poems "differ greatly in essential tone and outlook" (p. 116).

374. Cope, Jackson I. "Shakerly Marmion and Pope's *Rape of the Lock.*" *MLN*, LXXII (1957), 265–67.

Cites Shakerly Marmion's *Cupid and Psyche* as a source for "the elements of Belinda's dressing-table episode" (p. 267).

375. Copley, J. "*The Rape of the Lock*, II, 73–100," *MLN*, LXXVI (1961), 494–95.

Briefly comments on the repetitions and echoes "illustrated in Ariel's description of the various occupations of the sylphs" (p. 494).

376. Cunningham, Joseph S. *Pope: The Rape of the Lock.* Studies in English Literature, no. 2. Edited by David Daiches. London: Edward Arnold, 1961.

Explicates the poem, focusing on the function of the mock-epic, reversals of classical and social decorum, irony, parody, imagery, versification, and classical allusions. Cunningham also explains the characterization of the sylphs, Belinda, Clarissa, Thalestris, and the Baron. See also 200.

377. Davenport, A. "Florio and Pope," *N&Q*, CC (1955), 433.

Notes a "close verbal parallel" between *Rape of the Lock*, II, 27–28, and Florio's *Second Flutes.*

378. Field, P. J. "Marvell and *The Rape of the Lock,*" *N&Q*, XIV (1967), 408–9.

Suggests that *Rape of the Lock*, III, 161–70, may be indebted to Marvell's *Death of O.C.*, 281–86, and notes that the above lines as well as canto IV, 3–10, of *Rape of the Lock* reveal "the same development from a simple cumulative model [Marvell] to ironic juxtaposition."

379. Frost, William. "*The Rape of the Lock* and Pope's Homer," *MLQ*, VIII (1947), 342–54.

Discusses Pope's methods of composition, examines six passages in the poem which contain echoes of Pope's translations of Homer, and suggests the possibility that, after Pope wrote *Rape of the Lock* "in as heightened a style as he could command, he later added to the allusiveness of certain of his effects by surreptitious echoes newly dispersed through [the] *Iliad* and [the] *Odyssey*" (p. 353). See also 219.

380. Goggin, L. P. "La Caverne aux Vapeurs," *PQ*, XLII (1963), 404–11.

Offers a contrast between Desfontaines' and Voltaire's translations of the Cave of Spleen passage in *Rape of the Lock* and concludes that Voltaire's translation conveys accurately "the spirit of the original passage."

381. Golden, Samuel A. "Pope's *The Rape of the Lock,* III, 8," *Explicator*, XXII (1963), item 12.

Explains that line 8 ("and sometimes Tea") is a deliberate attempt by Pope "to keep in circulation the widespread rumor" of Queen Anne's "alleged intemperance."

382. Green-Armytage, A. H. N. "Ombre," *Spectator*, CLXXV (1945), 565.

Attacks Thomas Love Peacock's criticism in *Gryll Grange* that Pope incorrectly described the game of Ombre in *Rape of the Lock*. Green-Armytage closely examines Pope's description of the game and concludes that the account is accurate.

383. Hyman, Stanley Edgar. *Poetry and Criticism: Four Revolutions in Literary Taste*. New York: Atheneum, 1961.

Chapter three, "English Romanticism" (which first appeared in *HudR*, XIII [1960], 406–12), contains an explication of *Rape of the Lock*. Hyman focuses on the poem's symbolism and social implications.

384. Jack, Ian. " 'The True Raillery,' " *Cairo Studies in English* (1960), pp. 9–23.

Applies Sprat's and Shaftesbury's interpretations of "raillery" (satire as a "defence for *Good* and *Virtuous Works*") to Butler's *Hudibras*, Dryden's *MacFlecknoe*, and Pope's

Rape of the Lock and *Dunciad*. Jack finds that Pope's satires are examples of "true raillery" in that both poems teach as well as attack.

385. Jackson, James L. "Pope's *The Rape of the Lock* Considered as a Five-Act Epic," *PMLA*, LXV (1950), 1283–87.

Suggests that "Pope consciously or unconsciously relied on the well-known and conventional five-part dramatic structure of the Elizabethan dramatists and their successors for the organization of his expanded mock epic" (p. 1287).

386. *Julow, Victor. "The First Hungarian Translation of *The Rape of the Lock*," *Hungarian Studies in English*, I (1963), 19–24.

387. *Koziol, Herbert. "Alexander Popes Sylphen und William Congreves 'Incognita,' " *Anglia*, LXX (1952), 433–35.

388. Krieger, Murray. "The 'Frail China Jar' and the Rude Hand of Chaos," *CentR*, V (1961), 176–94.

Suggests a "dramatic relation" between *Rape of the Lock* and *Dunciad*, IV. Krieger focuses on an analysis of Pope's use of metonymy and zeugma in *Rape of the Lock*.

389. Lauter, Paul. "Belinda's Date," *CE*, XX (1959), 164–66.

Describes a method of teaching *Rape of the Lock* to adolescents, by discussing the parallels between the activities at Hampton Court and the modern practice of dating.

390. Mackenzie, M. L. "A New Dimension for *Tam O' Shanter*," *Studies in Scottish Literature*, I (October, 1963), 87–92.

Explains that the narrative poem *Tam O' Shanter* is also a mock-heroic poem which "echoes the technique and even the incidents of Pope's *The Rape of the Lock*."

391. Malarkey, Stoddard. "*The Rape of the Lock*, I, 16: A Chaucerian Parallel," *N&Q*, CCIX (1964), 55–56.

Finds a parallel between *Rape of the Lock*, I, 16, and Chaucer's *Troilus and Criseyde*, I, 920–21.

392. Moore, Frank Harper. "Dr. Pelling, Dr. Pell, and Dryden's Lord Nonsuch," *MLR*, XLIX (1954), 349–51.

Maintains that George Steevens' (1780) explanation of an allusion in *Rape of the Lock*, IV, 53, is not to Dr. Pelling, but to Dr. Pell who was also the model for Dryden's Lord Nonsuch.

393. Parkin, Rebecca Price. "Mythopoeic Activity in *The Rape of the Lock*," *ELH*, XXI (1954), 30–38.

Examines *Rape of the Lock*, stressing Pope's technique of integrating "a variety of established mythologies" (p. 38) such as Greek, Roman, Christian, Hebrew and Rosicrucian myths. Parkin states that the juxtaposition of "the Homeric and Christian myths helps suggest a spiritual approach to reality and particularly to human affairs, preparing the way for mythopoeic action" (p. 30).

394. ———. "Tension in Alexander Pope's Poetry," *UKCR*, XIX (1953), 169–73.

Studies the various types of tension utilized by Pope in *Rape of the Lock*, dialogue I of the *Epilogue to the Satires*, and *Temple of Fame*. See also 219.

395. Phillipson, John S. "Pope's 'Imprisoned Essences': An Unnoticed Metaphor," *AN&Q*, III (1965), 132–33.

Interprets the military image of line 94 of *Rape of the Lock*, II, as a continuation of "the implied figure of firearms."

396. Pittock, Malcolm. "*The Rape of the Lock*, I, 13–20," *N&Q*, CCXI (1966), 455–57.

Sees a flaw in lines 13–20 because of their ambiguous nature.

397. *Ploch, Richard A. "Abbé Nicolas de Montfaucon de Villars' *The Count de Gabalis, 1714*," *PBSA*, LVIII (3rd quarter, 1964), 279–81.

398. Pollard, Arthur. "*The Rape of the Lock*, III, 155–158," *N&Q*, CXCVII (1952), 363–64.

Argues that lines 155–58 reveal Pope's indebtedness to Dryden's translations of "The Nun's Priest's Tale" and the

Aeneid rather than Juvenal's *Saturae,* as suggested by Tillotson (see 20).

399. Preston, John. " 'Th' Informing Soul': Creative Irony in *The Rape of the Lock,*" *DUJ,* LVIII (1966), 125–30.

Interprets Pope's use of irony in *Rape of the Lock* and states that the poem's "irony has two dominant aspects": first, " 'a metaphor of tone' . . . Pope's way of defining his relationship to the social world" and, second, "the more openly 'satirical' aspect . . . in which Pope exposes the inner contradictions of that world" (p. 126).

400. Pyle, Fitzroy. "Six Notes on *The Rape of the Lock*: I—The 'Machinery,' " *N&Q,* CCII (1957), 252–54.

Suggests various sources for the machinery of the sylphs and four specific passages in *Rape of the Lock.*

401. Quintana, Ricardo. "*The Rape of the Lock* as a Comedy of Continuity," *REL,* vol. VII, no. 2 (1966), pp. 9–19.

Considers the poem as a "comedy of continuity—a comedy deriving . . . from a law of identity" with the dominant theme of transformation being concluded "in a paradoxical contradiction to the comedy of continuity."

402. Reichard, Hugo M. "The Love Affair in Pope's *Rape of the Lock,*" *PMLA,* LXIX (1954), 887-902.

Provides a detailed analysis of Belinda's character as an egotistical and proud "coquette." Reichard also discusses Pope's allusions to Milton, Virgil, and Shakespeare.

403. Riling, Mildred. " 'Puffs, Powders, Patches, Bibles, Billet-Doux,' " *N&Q,* CXCIV (1949), 537–38.

Argues against Tillotson's assertion (see 20) that the entire line, especially the satirical use of *Bibles,* has perplexed "inattentive readers." Riling maintains that "the sacrifice of sense to the intended satire has been too great" (p. 537) in Pope's use of the plural form of *Bibles.* See also 408.

404. *Schonhorn, Manuel R. "Pope's *Rape of the Lock,*" *AN&Q,* V (1967), 132–33.

405. Seronsy, Cecil C. "Dryden and Belinda's Toilet," *N&Q,* CXCVIII (1953), 28.

> Suggests that lines 599–600 of Dryden's translation of Juvenal's sixth satire may have been the model for *Rape of the Lock,* I, 133–34.

406. Sutherland, James R. *English Satire.* The Clark Lectures. Cambridge: At the University Press, 1958.

> Contains a brief analysis of *Rape of the Lock* and the *Dunciad* as examples of verse satire.

407. Sutherland, W. O. S., Jr. *The Art of the Satirist: Essays on the Satire of Augustan England.* Austin: University of Texas Press, 1965.

> Contrasts the 1712 edition of *Rape of the Lock* with its revision in five cantos in 1714 and concludes that Pope's "revisions are the difference between excellence and greatness" (p. 27).

408. Tillotson, Geoffrey. "Puffs, Powders, Patches, Bibles, and Billet-Doux," *N&Q,* CXCV (1950), 40–41.

> Answers Mildred Riling's interpretation of *Bibles* (see 403) by defending Pope's employment of the plural rather than the singular form of the word.

409. Wallace, Joel Wise. "The Augustan Poets and the Fair Sex." Unpublished Ph.D. dissertation, Columbia University, 1954, *DA,* XIV (1954), 1736.

> Considers Pope's "complex of responses and emotions" toward women as depicted by Belinda, who "represents the feminine paradox as Pope saw it."

410. Wasserman, Earl R. "The Limits of Allusion in *The Rape of the Lock,*" *JEGP,* LXV (1966), 425–44.

> Examines in detail the "Christian Greco-Roman," "classical-Scriptural" allusions in the poem. Wasserman concludes that "the rich interplay between the author's text and the full contexts it allusively arouses" are "functional" to the meaning of the poem (p. 444).

411. Williams, Aubrey L. "The 'Fall' of China and *The Rape of the Lock*," *PQ*, XLI (1962), 412–25.

Traces the tradition of "glass" imagery; analyzes the implications of the "vessel" imagery in canto II, 105–6, canto III, 157–60, and canto IV, 162–63; and suggests that the imagery indicates the "utter finality of the loss involved in the breaking of fine China, or of the frail bond of chastity" (p. 418). Williams also interprets Belinda's fall on the basis of the poem's parallels to *Paradise Lost* and "the parody of Sarpedon's speech in the *Iliad*" (p. 419). See also 219.

412. Wimsatt, William Kurtz, Jr. "The Game of Ombre in *The Rape of the Lock*," *RES*, n.s., I (1950), 136–43.

Provides a detailed analysis of the card game and concludes that the game is not completely or precisely described by Pope. Wimsatt maintains that hypothetical reconstructions of the game "have had no critical bearing on the poem" (p. 136) since "Pope's artistry depends . . . on what he has suppressed" (p. 139).

413. Zucker, David H. "The Detached and Judging Narrator in Chaucer's *House of Fame*," *Thoth*, vol. VIII, no. 1 (1967), pp. 3–22.

In section IV, Zucker compares Pope's Belinda with Chaucer's Fame and concludes that both poets, "by the irony of their narrative positions, put themselves in places of objective observation, producing ultimately judgment in us" (p. 22).

ELOISA TO ABELARD

414. Deeney, John Joseph, S.J. "A Critical Study of Alexander Pope's *Eloisa to Abelard.*" Unpublished Ph.D. dissertation, Fordham University, 1961, *DA*, XXII (1962), 4003–4.

Traces Pope's sources for the poem; surveys eighteenth-through twentieth-century critical opinion; examines the poem's "meter, imagery, allusions, irony, rhyme, personification, rhetorical devices, sound effects and the verse-paragraph" (p. 4003); and concludes that the extraordinary craftsmanship in the poem tends to disprove or modify the stereotyped concept of Pope's sterility and monotony.

415. Kalmey, Robert P. "Pope's *Eloisa to Abelard* and Those Celebrated Letters," *PQ*, XLVII (April, 1968), 164–78.

Analyzes "the basic Christian fabric of the poem in an effort to discover some of the ways by which a 'careful cultivation' helps to create, out of a collection of old letters, a new poem. . . ." Kalmey concludes that a "new hierarchical order of love" is established with "Abelard the man as priest, the agent of God, (who) supports the new order of Eloisa's love—a love that now embraces first God, and then Abelard the sanctified man" (p. 178).

416. *Mandel, Barrett J. "Pope's *Eloisa to Abelard*," *TSLL*, IX (1967), 57–68.

417. O'Hehir, Brendan P. "Virtue and Passion: The Dialectic of *Eloisa to Abelard*," *TSLL*, II (1960), 219–32.

Explicates *Eloisa to Abelard,* focusing on a defense of the poem's structure. O'Hehir cautions critics against assuming that Pope is the speaker or persona of the poem, reveals that there are natural explanations for the "pathetic fallacies" in the poem, and concludes that the poem's "effects are calculated [and] its confusion not without a plan" (p. 232). See also 219.

418. Pettit, Henry. "Pope's *Eloisa to Abelard*: An Interpretation," University of Colorado Studies: Series in Language and Literature, no. 4, July, 1953, pp. 67–74.

Examines *Eloisa to Abelard* as an "elegiac lyric" and studies the philosophical temper and the structure of the poem as well as the character of the heroine. Pettit states that "pathetic fallacy is supreme and sentiment surges for expression" (p. 71) in the poem. See also 219.

419. Pope, Alexander. *Eloisa to Abelard. With the letters of Heloise to Abelard in the version by John Hughes (1713)*. Introduction and notes by James E. Wellington. University of Miami Critical Studies, no. 5. Coral Gables: University of Miami Press, 1965.

Wellington's introduction is divided into three parts: part I, a detailed biography of Abelard and Heloise; part II, a bibliographical note; and part III, a detailed critical analysis of the poem. Also included is the "actual source" from which Pope worked, the Hughes version of the letters from Heloise to Abelard, and complete cross-referencing in Wellington's notes.

420. Aden, John M. "Texture and Structure in Pope: A Dissent," *CE*, XIX (1958), 358.

> Disagrees with Robert H. Zoellner (see 475). Aden argues that Pope's use of the heroic couplet does not enforce the Chain of Being idea in *Essay on Man*.

421. *Beaumont, Charles A. "The Rising and Falling Metaphor in Pope's *An Essay on Man*," *Style*, I (1967), 127–30.

422. Boyce, Benjamin. "Baroque into Satire: Pope's Frontispiece for the *Essay on Man*," *Criticism*, IV (1962), 14–27.

> Provides twelve plates, two of the frontispiece to *Essay on Man* and ten of eighteenth-century capriccio. Boyce interprets Pope's engraving; compares it with the capriccio tradition; reveals Pope's debt to the tradition; and suggests Pope's possible debt to Owen MacSwiny's *Tombeaux*, "a series of baroque, honorific tomb-pictures" (p. 22).

423. Brett, Reginald L. "Pope's *Essay on Man*," *Reason and Imagination: A Study of Form and Meaning in Four Poems*. London: Oxford University Press for University of Hull, 1960.

> States that, although Bolingbroke influenced Pope, the latter did not simply versify the former's philosophy. Brett compares Bolingbroke's philosophy with Pope's, discusses the philosophical sources of the essay and the role of nature, and focuses on the philosophical and poetical structure of the poem.

> Reviewed by Bonamy Dobrée, *CritQ*, II (1960), 89, 91–92; H. A. Smith, *MLR*, LVI (1961), 237; George Whalley, *DR*, XLI (1961), 246–48.

424. Bullough, Geoffrey. "Changing Views of the Mind in English Poetry," *PBA*, XLI (1955), 61–83.

> Contains a brief reference to Pope's theory of the ruling passion in *Essay on Man*.

425. *Cameron, Allen B. "Pope's *An Essay on Man*, IV, 249–252," *Explicator*, XXVI (1967), item 23.

426. Cameron, J. M. "Doctrinal to an Age: Notes Towards a Revaluation of Pope's *Essay on Man*," *Dublin Review*, 2d quarter, 1951, pp. 54–69.

> Examines Pope's philosophy as expressed in *Essay on Man*, discusses Pope's method of composition, and disagrees on various points of interpretation with Maynard Mack's explication of the poem (14). See also 219.

427. Cruttwell, Patrick. "Pope and His Church," *HudR*, XIII (1960), 392–405.

> Studies Pope's attitude toward Catholicism as revealed in his correspondence and *Essay on Man*. Cruttwell states that Pope was a "Catholic but not a Papist" (p. 403) and that Pope was "very anxious to dissociate himself from . . . fellow-Catholics who still believed that their faith obliged them to revolutionary (Jacobite) politics" (p. 403).

428. De Mordaunt, Walter J. "Ransom, Pope, and the Intentional Fallacy," *CE*, XX (1959), 415.

> Challenges John M. Aden's rebuttal (see 420) to Robert H. Zoellner's views on *Essay on Man* (see 475) and explains John Crowe Ransom's definition of texture.

429. Dixon, Peter. "Pope's *An Essay on Man*, II, 181–194," *Explicator*, XXIII (1964), item 21.

> Demonstrates the consistency of the word *strainers* in the garden image of lines 181–94.

430. Dobrée, Bonamy. "Books and Writers," *Spectator*, CLXXXVI (1951), 418.

> Comments on the philosophical ideas and the structure of *Essay on Man* and provides a brief statement regarding the *Moral Essays*.

431. Fabian, Bernhard. "A Reference to Pope's *Essay on Man*," *N&Q*, CCII (1957), 269–70.

> Identifies a letter reprinted by Vedder M. Gilbert (see

484) as referring to Pope's *Essay on Man*, which Fabian claims "has to be dated according to the New Style, March 13, 1733" (p. 269).

432. Fabian, Bernhard. "Pope's 'Half-reas'ning Elephant,'" *N&Q*, CCX (1965), 451–52.

> Suggests Giovanni Battista Gelli's *Circe* (1549) as a possible source for line 222 of *Essay on Man*, I.

433. *————. "Zur Morallehre in Alexander Popes *Essay on Man*," *Germanisch-Romanische Monatsschrift*, VII (1957), 290–97.

434. Faley, Brother Roland. "Pope's *Essay on Man*, I, 294," *Explicator*, IX (1951), item 51.

> States that Pope's "Whatever is, is right" must be explicated on the basis of "goodness" in its ontological sense.

435. Fleischmann, Wolfgang Bernard. "Alexander Pope and Lucretian 'Anonymity,'" *Neophilologus*, XLIV (1960), 216–18.

> Considers the literary influence of the ideas and style of Lucretius' *De Rerum Natura* on Pope's *Essay on Man*, I.

436. Foxon, David F. *Thomas J. Wise and the Pre-Restoration Drama: A Study in Theft and Sophistication*. London: The Bibliographical Society, 1959.

> States that an "uncut copy of the first edition of Pope's *Essay on Man* in the Ashley Library was stolen (except for the title) from the [British] museum" (p. 1).

437. Fraser, Russell A. "Pope and Shakespeare," *SAQ*, LIX (1960), 88–102.

> Compares the theological and philosophical aspect of man and his relationship to God in Pope's *Essay on Man* with that of Shakespeare's plays. Fraser concludes that Pope "contrived" in his essay to subvert "all that he stood for" (p. 102).

438. Frost, William. "Pope's *Essay on Man*, I, 95–113," *Explicator*, VI (1947), item 11.

Studies the Indian passage on the basis of its ironical implications which are "in favor of the Indian on moral as well as intellectual terms."

439. Goldgar, Bertrand A. "Pope's Theory of the Passions: The Background of Epistle II of the *Essay on Man*," *PQ*, XLI (1962), 730–43.

Investigates the background of the ethical and psychological theories of the passions, analyzes Pope's justification and application of the theory, and asserts that Pope's "procedure of showing partial ill to be universal good is Pope's doctrine of the ruling passion" (p. 739).

440. *Grabes, Herbert. "Die rhetorische Struktur von Popes *Essay on Man*," *Anglia*, LXXXIV (1966), 353–87.

441. Greene, Donald J. " 'Logical Structure' in Eighteenth-Century Poetry," *PQ*, XXXI (1952), 315–36.

Comments that *Essay on Man* has "no real logical order . . . beyond that of simple enumeration" (p. 330). Greene also finds that the structure of the *Epistle to Dr. Arbuthnot* does not resemble a "logically constructed treatise" (p. 331).

442. Hart, James D. *The Popular Book: A History of America's Literary Taste*. New York: Oxford University Press, 1950.

Briefly discusses the availability, purchase, and reading of Pope's works, especially his *Essay on Man*, in America during the middle and late eighteenth century. Hart states that forty-five editions of the essay "were printed in America between 1747 and 1799" and that Pope was widely read and quoted.

443. Hart, John Forest. "A Reading of Alexander Pope's Moral Poetry: The Epistles and Satires of the 1730's." Unpublished Ph.D. dissertation, University of Washington, 1967, *DA*, XXVIII (1967), 1786.

Examines *Essay on Man*, *Epistles to Several Persons*, and *Imitations of Horace* in order to "evaluate the impact of [the] *Essay*'s moral-philosophical position on the *Epistles* and the *Imitations*."

444. Hughes, Richard Edward. "Pope's *Essay on Man*: The Rhetorical Structure of Epistle I," *MLN*, LXX (1955), 177–81.

> Examines Pope's "deliberate use of the traditional oratorical framework" (p. 177) for rhetorical persuasion: *exordium, narratio, probatio, refutatio,* and *peroratio.* See also 219.

445. Jones, William Powell. "Newton Further Demands the Muse," *SEL*, III (1963), 287–306.

> States that Pope's *Essay on Man* reflects the influence of Newton's *Principia* ("orderly universe idea") "rather than the beauty of light and colors shown in the *Optics.*"

446. ———. "The Idea of the Limitations of Science from Prior to Blake," *SEL*, I (1961), 97–114.

> Briefly comments on *Essay on Man* as a treatment of the dichotomy between science and theology and as a summary of "the physico-theological thinking of the decade after Newton's death" (p. 98).

447. Kallich, Martin. *Heav'n's First Law: Rhetoric and Order in Pope's Essay on Man.* De Kalb: Northern Illinois University Press, 1967.

> Attempts "to show how the antithesis . . . has been used to integrate the total poem and to provide certain special esthetic effects"; studies "repeated words and ideas . . . to show how Pope develops his argument and . . . unifies the philosophy underlying the structure of the total poem"; examines "repeated imagery and attempts to reveal a pattern—the circular frame." Kallich concludes that "Pope is lavish in his use of detail . . . and unites judgment and fancy in a decorous and seemly union."

448. ———. "Pope's *An Essay on Man*, II, 175–194," *Explicator*, XXV (1966), item 17.

> Discusses the thematic function of the garden image in lines 175–94.

449. ———. "Pope's 'Green Myriads in the Peopled Grass,'" *N&Q*, CCXI (1966), 214.

> Interprets line 210 of *Essay on Man*, I.

450. Kallich, Martin. "The Conversation and the Frame of Love: Images of Unity in Pope's *Essay on Man*," *PLL*, II (Winter, 1966), 21–37.

> Finds "two large focal images" sustained throughout the essay. The first image maintains "a dramatic point of view" by introducing itself as a conversation between friends and between pupil and instructor; however, the second image, that of a "circular frame," encloses "an infinite series of ever-decreasing circles" and finally comes to a point.

451. ————. "Thomas Gray's Annotations to Pope's *Essay on Man*," *N&Q*, CCX (1965), 454–55.

> Prints three annotations of a first edition of Pope's *Essay on Man*, presumably written by Thomas Gray.

452. *————. "Unity and Dialectic: The Structural Role of Antithesis in Pope's *Essay on Man*," *PLL*, I (1965), 109–24.

453. Laird, John. *Philosophical Incursions into English Literature*. Cambridge: At the University Press, 1946.

> Contains a chapter on Pope's *Essay on Man* in which Laird analyzes the philosophical content of each of the four epistles of the essay. Laird contrasts Bolingbroke's philosophy with that of Pope and concludes that Pope did not consistently follow Bolingbroke's philosophy.

454. Lawlor, Nancy K. "Pope's *Essay on Man:* Oblique Light for a False Mirror," *MLQ*, vol. XXVIII, no. 3 (1967), pp. 305–16.

> Analyzing the poem's orthodoxy, Lawlor discusses "the ironic implications of the poem's Christian-deistic ambiguity" and concludes that Pope absorbs "deistic naturalism into the Christian concept of Divine Order" and substantiates "that 'natural' theology itself leans on and proves the necessity of revealed truth" (p. 313).

455. Litz, Francis E. "Pope's Use of Derham," *JEGP*, LX (1961), 65–74.

> Provides an analysis of William Derham's *Physico-Theology* (1713) and *Astro-Theology* (1715) as sources for a number of passages in Pope's *Essay on Man*.

456. Macklem, Michael. *The Anatomy of the World: Relations Between Natural and Moral Law from Donne to Pope.* Minneapolis: University of Minnesota Press, 1958.

Explicates *Essay on Man* in terms of the philosophical and theological concepts of natural and moral evil suggested in the poem.

457. Manley, Francis. "Pope's *An Essay on Man,* IV, 121–130," *Explicator,* XV (April, 1957), item 44.

Examines lines 121–30 and states that the passage is an example of "Pope's most complex satiric irony."

458. Medford, Floyd. "The *Essay on Man* and the *Essay on the Origin of Evil,*" *N&Q,* CXCIV (1949), 337–38.

Maintains that since Edmund Law's English translation of Archbishop King's *Essay on the Origin of Evil* appeared in November of 1730, and not in 1731, Pope could conceivably have employed the English translation rather than the Latin original.

459. Monk, Samuel Holt. " 'Die of a Rose': *Essay on Man,* I, 199–200," *HLQ,* XXI (1958), 359–61.

States that lines 199–200 echo the structure of Lady Winchilsea's ode, "The Spleen," and reflect the scientific precision of Robert Boyle's *Essays of the Strange Subtilty, Great Efficacy, and Determinate Nature of Effluviums.*

460. Moran, Berna. "Pope and Thomas Vaughan," *TLS,* May 4, 1951, p. 277.

Suggests the probability that Pope read a poem in Thomas Vaughan's treatise *Anthroposophia Theomagica.* Moran notes an "interesting resemblance" between the first two lines of Vaughan's poem and Pope's *Essay on Man,* II, 1–2.

461. Pollard, Arthur. "Five Poets on Religion. 1. Dryden, Pope, and Young. 2. Cowper and Blake," *CQR,* CLX (1959), 352–62, 436–45.

Examines the Christian orthodoxy in *Essay on Man.*

462. Priestley, F. E. L. "Pope and the Great Chain of Being,"

Essays in English Literature from the Renaissance to the Victorian Age Presented to A. S. P. Woodhouse. Edited by Millar MacLure and F. W. Watt. Toronto: University of Toronto Press, 1964.

Argues that "none of the *Essay on Man* is constructed around the Great Chain of Being as a main constitutive idea" (p. 227). Priestley discusses the difference between Pope's and Leibniz's doctrines and examines those elements of the tradition of the Great Chain which Pope does not express. See also 223.

463. Rogers, Robert W. "Critiques of the *Essay on Man* in France and Germany, 1736–1755," *ELH*, xv (1948), 176–93.

Outlines "the major critiques demonstrating various heterodox features of Pope's argument" (p. 176); studies the "extent to which Pope came to be accepted primarily as a *philosophe*" (p. 176); and examines Gotthold Lessing' and Moses Mendelssohn's *Pope ein Metaphysiker!* Rogers states that "the aesthetic merits of the *Essay on Man* were largely ignored in print, while the validity of its ideas, the logic of its argument, and the exactness of its phrasing were tested by prevailing religious and philosophic views" (p. 176).

Reviewed by James Edward Tobin, *PQ*, xxviii (1949), 398–99.

464. ———. "The Early Vogue of the *Essay on Man*," *Harvard University Graduate School of Arts and Sciences. Summaries of Theses.* Cambridge: Harvard University Press, 1946.

Pages 281–84 contain a summary of Rogers' dissertation which was written in 1942. Rogers examines the eighteenth-century criticism of *Essay on Man* and determines its significance. Rogers also classifies the criticism under three categories: "discussion of the philosophy in the poem, praise for Pope as a moralist, and imitations of his content and poetical manner" (p. 282).

465. ———. "Notes on Pope's Collaboration with Warburton in Preparing a Final Edition of the *Essay on Man*," *PQ*, xxvi (1947), 358–66.

Compares the 1739 and 1744 editions in order to determine the extent of Warburton's influence in suggesting "modifications to bring the poem more in line with contemporary orthodox sentiment" (p. 358). Rogers examines changes in phraseology and lines added or omitted which "possibly modify or alter the doctrine [or] indicate . . . possible shifts in crucial points of doctrine" (p. 359).

466. Simon, Irène. " 'Pride of Reason' in the Restoration and Earlier Eighteenth Century," *Revue des Langues Vivantes,* XXV (1959), 375–96.

Mentions that Pope rejected the "pride of meddling intellect" in *Essay on Man.*

467. ———. "Shaftesbury and Eighteenth-Century Poetry," *Revue des Langues Vivantes,* XXVII (1961), 200–215.

Contains a brief reference to Pope's appeal to reason and his "poetic form" in *Essay on Man.*

468. Sparrow, John. *Independent Essays.* London: Faber & Faber, 1963.

In chapter four, Sparrow provides a general discussion of why Pope's *Essay on Man* fails as a system of philosophy and as a poem.

Reviewed in *TLS,* June 28, 1963, p. 478.

469. Troy, Frederick S. "Pope's Images of Man," *Massachusetts Review,* I (1960), 359–84.

Argues that Maynard Mack's interpretation of *Essay on Man* (see 14) as "thoroughly traditional" can not be substantiated since the poem "represents a radical departure" from the "Renaissance classical impulse" (p. 360). In order to illustrate his interpretation, Troy provides a detailed analysis of "Pope's treatment of the idea of the law of nature" (p. 362).

470. Tuveson, Ernest. "*An Essay on Man* and 'The Way of Ideas,' " *ELH,* XXVI (1959), 368–86.

Describes the extensive influence of the Lockean "revolution in epistemology," briefly explains Locke's philosophy, and explicates aspects of Pope's essay which reveal "the moral and philosophical-religious results of the Lockean revolution" (p. 375). See also 471.

Reviewed by Robert Marsh, *PQ*, XXXIX (1960), 349–51.

471. Tuveson, Ernest. *"An Essay on Man* and 'The Way of Ideas': Some Further Remarks," *PQ*, XL (1961), 262–69.

Defends his interpretation of Locke's influence on Pope challenged by Robert Marsh's review (see 470). Tuveson asserts that Pope had read Locke's *Essay concerning the Human Understanding* and that Lockean epistemology was discussed by Pope and was reflected in "the intellectual atmosphere in which Pope composed *An Essay on Man*" (p. 266).

472. Wasser, Henry. "Pope's *An Essay on Man,* I, 16," *Explicator*, VII (1948), item 12.

Suggests that "Pope in his endeavor to bring a rationalistic formulation to his moral beliefs uses the explanatory 'vindicate' in lieu of the more direct 'justifie' in borrowing Milton's celebrated line."

473. Williams, Edward Kneale. "The Decline of Optimism in Eighteenth-Century England (Parts I–IV)." Unpublished Ph.D. dissertation, Cornell University, 1956, *DA*, XVI (1956), 2451–52.

Traces the etymology of optimism from classical times through Pope's *Essay on Man*. Williams concludes that "the paradoxical moral imperatives in Pope's system—those of submitting to the lessons of nature, and of striving to attain, through analogical reasoning, a view of the whole— were not lost in the transition to the romantic period" (p. 2451).

474. Wronker, Stanley S. "Pope and Ben Jonson," *N&Q*, CXCVI (1951), 495–96.

Suggests that *Essay on Man,* II, 18, is a "deliberate parody" of a line in Ben Jonson's "To the Memory of My Beloved, the Author Mr. William Shakespeare."

475. Zoellner, Robert H. "Poetic Cosmology in Pope's *An Essay on Man*," *CE*, XIX (1958), 157–62.

Divides Pope's structural ideas in epistle I into the following groups: "the principle of gradation . . . which receives explicit statement in the image of the Great Chain of Being" (p. 157) ; a combination of the preceding idea with Newton's concept of a "spherical" universe; the concept of man's duality because of his position as the middle link in the Chain; and Pope's concept of balance. Zoellner finds that the syntactical arrangement and the imagery within epistle I support Pope's structural ideas, that is, the "texture" of the poem reinforces its "structure." See also 420 and 428.

MORAL ESSAYS

476. Alpers, Paul J. "Pope's *To Bathurst* and the Mandevillian State," *ELH*, xxv (1958), 23–42.

Disagrees with W. J. Courthope's (*Works of Alexander Pope*, 1881) and G. Wilson Knight's (see 216) interpretations of Pope's epistle. Alpers maintains that *To Bathurst* is in direct opposition to the ethical assumptions made by Mandeville in his *Fable of the Bees* and that the poem is not a "moral essay," nor does it contain any "sort of primitivism" (p. 30). Alpers provides a detailed explication of Pope's "Horatian epistle," stressing the poem's theme, "philosophical core," and character-portraits. See also 219.

477. Altenbernd, A. Lynn. "On Pope's 'Horticultural Romanticism,'" *JEGP*, LIV (1955), 470–77.

Considers the development of English gardening and Pope's theory of gardening as expressed in his works (specifically the section on gardening in *Epistle to Burlington*). Altenbernd concludes that "there is no real contradiction between his neoclassicism as a poet and his theory and practice as a gardener" (p. 471) since the "grounds at Twickenham represented not so much a reaction against the formal garden itself as against its excesses . . ." (p. 476). See also 219.

478. Butt, John. "'A Master Key to Popery,'" *Pope and His Contemporaries: Essays Presented to George Sherburn*. Edited by James L. Clifford and Louis A. Landa. Oxford: Clarendon Press, 1949.

Prints an unpublished prose pamphlet transcribed by Lady Burlington entitled "A Master Key to Popery." Butt discusses the background, publication, and authorship of the pamphlet (which was a defense of Pope's *Epistle to Burlington*) and concludes that it was written by Pope. See also 186.

479. Crawford, Charlotte E. "What Was Pope's Debt to Edward Young?" *ELH*, xiii (1946), 157–67.

Examines the extent to which the tone, diction, moral,

theme, subject matter, and character-portraits of the *Moral
Essays* reflect Pope's indebtedness to Young's Horatian
style.

480. Daniels, Elizabeth Adams. "Pope's *Moral Essays* and
'Tulipomania,'" *N&Q,* CCIV (1959), 397–98.

> Explicates lines 41–44 of epistle II on the basis of a recent
> scientific discovery of Dr. René J. Dubos on "the breeding
> of tulips in relation to virology" (p. 398).

481. Edwards, Thomas Robert, Jr. "'Reconcil'd Extremes':
Pope's *Epistle to Bathurst,*" *EIC,* XI (1961), 290–308.

> Studies *Epistle to Bathurst,* focusing on the poem's theme,
> the function of the character-portraits, and the epistle's
> stress on exposing "the growing confusion between wealth
> and moral value" (p. 291). In the appendix to his article,
> Edwards argues against Earl R. Wasserman's interpreta-
> tion (see 491) of "Pope's role in the poem [as] a funda-
> mentally and profoundly Christian one" (p. 306).

482. Erskine-Hill, Howard H. "The Lucky Hit in Commerce
and Creation: Atterbury and Pope's Sir Balaam," *N&Q,*
XIV (1967), 407–8.

> Explains the significance of line 378 of *Epistle to Bathurst*
> as an echo of Atterbury's *Miraculous Propagation of the
> Gospel* (1694).

483. ———. "The Medal against Time: A Study of Pope's
Epistle To Mr. Addison," *Journal of the Warburg and Courtauld Institutes,* XXVIII (1965), 274–98.

> Provides a detailed analysis of the content and structure
> of the poem "in relation to the relevant background of ideas"
> (p. 276). Erskine-Hill concludes that the poem "is central
> to an understanding of Pope's conception of his own age
> and its relation to classical antiquity" (p. 298).

484. Gilbert, Vedder M. "Unrecorded Comments on John Gay,
Henry Travers, and Others," *N&Q,* CXCVIII (1953), 337–39.

> Prints a letter by Thomas Edwards of Terrick which
> indicates that London was reading Pope's *Epistle to
> Bathurst,* and "A Letter to the Imitator of Horace" sup-
> posed to have been composed by Lady Mary. See also 431.

485. Hibbard, G. R. "The Country House Poem of the Seven-

teenth Century," *Essential Articles for the Study of Alexander Pope.* Edited by Maynard Mack. Hamden, Conn.: Shoestring Press, 1964.

Describes in detail seventeenth-century English domestic architecture and discusses the "character and function of the large country house"; analyzes the country-house tradition in the poetry of Ben Jonson, Thomas Carew, Herrick, and Marvell; and examines the basic ideas of this tradition in Pope's *Epistle to Burlington,* specifically in Pope's attack on Chandos' house, "Cannons." Hill also attacks F. W. Bateson's criticism of *Epistle to Burlington,* contending that "Pope's criticism of society is fundamentally moral" (p. 431) and that his attack is a coherent criticism on "human pride" and man's failure to use his house in relationship to his society and his natural world. Also published in *Journal of the Warburg and Courtauld Institutes,* XIX (1956), 159–74.

486. Levine, Jay Arnold. "Pope's *Epistle to Augustus,* Lines 1–30," *SEL,* VII (Summer, 1967), 426–51.

Finds motifs in the exordium which dominate and control the theme and states that Pope employed, for satiric purposes, beliefs of the Christian humanist tradition. Levine also provides a detailed explication of the exordium.

487. Mabbott, Thomas O. "Pope's *Moral Essays, Epistle V* (To Mr. Addison, Occasioned by His Dialogue on Medals)," *Explicator,* X (1951), item 11.

Examines, "from the viewpoint of a numismatist," those passages in epistle v which deal with medals or ancient coins.

488. Parkin, Rebecca Price. "The Role of Time in Alexander Pope's *Epistle to a Lady,*" *ELH,* XXXII (1965), 490–501.

Provides a detailed explication of Pope's *Epistle to a Lady: Of the Characters of Women.* Parkin concludes that the poem simultaneously maintains "two interpenetrating paradoxes—one regarding time and the other regarding ethics."

489. *Schafer, Robert G. "Cannons No Canon: Pope's *Epistle to Burlington,*" *PMASAL,* XLV (1959), 403–10.

490. Schonhorn, Manuel R. "Pope's *Epistle to Augustus* and Ambrose Philips," *N&Q,* XIV (1967) 406–7.

Discusses lines 417–18 of the epistle as clearly referring to Eusden and Settle, and possibly to Philips since Pope may also have had in mind two panegyrics written by Philips.

491. Wasserman, Earl R. *Pope's Epistle to Bathurst: A Critical Reading with an Edition of the Manuscripts.* Baltimore: Johns Hopkins Press, 1960.

In his explication of the epistle, Wasserman asserts that the "control of the satiric and Christian tones" in the poem are due to "a set of complexly acting and interacting attitudes" which are derived from Pope's "tone or voice" or "climate of attitudes" (p. 11). Wasserman includes the text of the epistle and a reproduction of the first edition which contains thirty facsimiles of the manuscript. See also 176 and 481.

Reviewed by Robert M. Schmitz, *PQ,* XL (1961), 418–20; Robert W. Rogers, *JEGP,* LXI (1962), 408–10; Jacques Golliet, *EA,* XVI (1963), 83–84; William Kurtz Wimsatt, Jr., *MLR,* LVIII (1963), 103–4; Norman Callan, *RES,* n.s., XV (1964), 92–94; Bernhard Fabian, *Anglia,* LXXXI (1963), 250–56.

492. Wellington, James E. "Pope and Charity," *PQ,* XLVI (1967), 225–35.

Studies the contrast between Pope's and his society's attitudes toward poverty and employs passages from Pope's *Epistle to Bathurst* and translation of Homer to clarify the poet's biblical conception of poverty and charity: (1) "poverty . . . is not necessarily a crime springing from individual indolence and vice, and (2) that the charity which relieves poverty is a corporal work of mercy . . ." (p. 234).

EPISTLE TO DR. ARBUTHNOT

493. Aden, John M. "A Pope Alteration Explained," *N&Q*, CCXI (1966), 212–13.

>   Offers an explanation for the difference in two versions of lines 289–304 of Pope's *Epistle to Dr. Arbuthnot.*

494. Brown, Wallace Cable. "Dramatic Tension in Neoclassic Satire," *CE*, VI (1945), 263–69.

>   States that the satires of Dryden, Pope, Johnson, and Churchill do not lack dramatic tension. Brown examines Pope's *Epistle to Dr. Arbuthnot* as an example of controlled patterns of dramatic tension.

495. Crossett, John. "Bishop Hall and Pope's Portrait of Atticus," *N&Q*, CCVI (1961), 253.

>   Suggests that Pope's portrait of Atticus in *Epistle to Dr. Arbuthnot* (lines 197–208) echoes Bishop Joseph Hall's sketch "Of the Envious."

496. Dixon, Peter. "The Theme of Friendship in the *Epistle to Dr. Arbuthnot,*" *ES*, XLIV (1963), 191–97.

>   Examines the theme of friendship and personal relations in conjunction with Pope's portrayal of Arbuthnot as an "impartial character reference," a "good friend," whose juxtaposition with "false friends and flatterers" provides Pope with "a satiric point of reference, and a guarantee of Pope's good character" (p. 192).

497. Dodd, Betty Coshow. "Pope's *Epistle to Dr. Arbuthnot,* 305–333," *Explicator*, XIX (1960), item 17.

>   Explains that the characterization of Sporus is not only a lampoon on Pope's personal enemy, but is also a satiric treatment of Hervey as a dunce.

498. Fleischmann, Wolfgang Bernard. "A Note on Spenser and Pope," *N&Q*, CXCIX (1954), 16–17.

>   Indicates that there is a "striking resemblance" between lines 340–41 of *Epistle to Dr. Arbuthnot* and Spenser's

"Proem" to the *Faerie Queene*, I, despite a "more proximate model for his line" in Matthew Prior's "Ode to the Queen."

499. Mack, Maynard. "Some Annotations in the Second Earl of Oxford's Copies of Pope's *Epistle to Dr. Arbuthnot* and *Sober Advice from Horace*," *RES*, n.s., VIII (1957), 416–20.

Contends that two annotations previously attributed to Lord Oxford were written by Pope. Mack also defends Oxford's interpretation of an allusion in line 121 of *Sober Advice*.

500. Maxwell, J. C. "Sporus and Patroclus," *RES*, XXIV (1948), 141.

Cites *Troilus and Cressida* (v, i, 34ff.) to prove Pope's indebtedness for his characterization of Hervey in *Epistle to Dr. Arbuthnot*, 305–10.

501. Meagher, John C. " 'Sporus, That Mere White Curd of Ass's Milk,' " *N&Q*, CCXI (1966), 460.

States that Pope's allusion to Lord Hervey as "Ass's Milk," in *Epistle to Dr. Arbuthnot*, is a variation on the theme of the effeminacy of Lord Hervey.

502. Mengel, Elias F., Jr. "Patterns of Imagery in Pope's *Arbuthnot*," *PMLA*, LXIX (1954), 189–97.

Provides an analysis of the unifying patterns of imagery in the poem. Mengel finds that "five main images emerge, all connected in a kind of evolution: animal—filth—disease —persecution—virtuous man" (p. 189). See also 219.

503. Rawson, C. J. "Pope's Echoes in Byron's *To Romance* and *Don Juan*, IV, 3," *N&Q*, CCXI (1966), 179.

Draws a parallel to Pope's *Epistle to Dr. Arbuthnot*, 340–41.

504. Weinbrot, Howard D. "Prior Helps Pope to 'Moralize His Song,' " *N&Q*, CCXI (1966), 459.

Notes an exact parallel of line 341 of Pope's *Epistle to Dr. Arbuthnot* to the final couplet of the first stanza of Prior's *Ode Humbly Inscribed to the Majesty's Arms, 1706*.

SATIRES

505. Aden, John M. "Pope and the Satiric Adversary," *SEL*, II (1962), 267–86.

> Examines the use of the *adversarius*, or interlocutor, in the satiric dialogues of Horace, Juvenal, and Persius, and in the Horatian verse satires of Pope. See also 219.

506. Bloom, Lillian D. "Pope as Textual Critic: A Bibliographical Study of His Horatian Text," *JEGP*, XLVII (1948), 150–55.

> Reviews Pope's attitude toward Bentley as a person and as an editor of Horace, cites the various editions of Horace that Pope had access to, provides an analysis of Pope's edition as compared with three other Horatian texts, and concludes that "Pope's Horatian text emerges finally as an eclectic text, based largely on the vulgate readings preserved by Heinsius and occasionally emended by the most substantial of the Bentley variants" (p. 152). See also 219.

507. Boyette, Purvis, E. "Pope's *Epilogue to the Satires, Dialogue,* II, 171–182," *Explicator*, XXIV (1965), item 46.

> Argues that the Westphaly Hogs simile functions as the "ethical crux" of dialogue II.

508. *Bross, Addison C. "Alexander Pope's Revisions of John Donne's *Satyres,*" *Xavier University Studies*, V (1966), 133–52.

509. Connolly, Cyril. *The Condemned Playground: Essays, 1927–1944.* New York: Macmillan, 1946.

> Comments in a brief essay on Pope's "defects" in *Imitations of Horace* and *Epistle to Dr. Arbuthnot*.

510. Dixon, Peter. "Pope, George Ogle, and Horace," *N&Q*, CCIV (1959), 396–97.

> Suggests that Pope, in his *First Epistle of the First Book*, may have been influenced by George Ogle's *Epistles of Horace Imitated* (1735).

511. Dixon, Peter. "Pope's 'Rich Widows,'" *N&Q*, CCVII (1962), 248–49.

Explicates lines 124–33 of Pope's *First Epistle of the First Book of Horace Imitated.*

512. Dupree, Robert Scott. "Boileau and Pope: The Horatian Perspective in France and England." Unpublished Ph.D. dissertation, Yale University, 1966, *DA*, XXVII (1966), 2496–97.

Compares and contrasts the Horatian mode of satire of both Boileau and Pope. Dupree concludes that "Boileau's twelfth satire and Pope's *Dunciad* are the last productions of two men who had begun with dreams of witnessing the rebirth of Rome's golden age and who ended by recognizing the impossibility of reviving the Horatian perspective in a declining world."

513. Edwards, Thomas Robert, Jr. "Heroic Folly: Pope's Satiric Identity," *In Defense of Reading.* Edited by Reuben Arthur Brower and Richard Poirier. New York: Dutton, 1962.

Explicates the first two dialogues from the *Epilogue to the Satires.* Edwards focuses on the heroic and moral identity of Pope in the context of social alienation since Pope, the satirist, does not offer an alternative to the morally perverted order he angrily denounces.

514. Hagedorn, Ralph. "Pope and Horace," *N&Q*, CXCIV (1949), 144–45.

States that the Elzevir edition of 1629 may have been the edition used by Pope for *Imitations of Horace.*

515. Hambrick, Thomas Gregory. "Satire as Apologia: An Analysis of the Chief Modes of Rhetorical Proof in the Apologetic Satires of Alexander Pope." Unpublished Ph.D. dissertation, University of Illinois, 1961, *DA*, XXII (1962), 3774–75.

Examines the chief modes of rhetorical proof in Pope's satires written in the Horatian manner (including *Epistle to Dr. Arbuthnot*).

516. Hughes, Richard Edward. "Pope's *Imitations of Horace* and the Ethical Focus," *MLN,* LXXI (1956), 569–74.

Cites passages from Pope's *Imitations* as a basis for discussing one of his satiric techniques: ethical focus. Hughes explains that in "Pope's ethical defense of himself and his satire" (p. 570), he manipulates Horace's intentions by redirecting Horace's account of virtues to himself.

517. Hunter, G. K. "Pope's Imitations of Fanshawe," *N&Q,* CCIV (1959), 193–94.

Cites close parallels between Sir Richard Fanshawe's translation of the *First Satire of the Second Book of Horace* and Pope's "imitation" of the same poem, and raises the question whether Pope deliberately consulted Fanshawe or whether Pope simply knew enough of the latter "to affect his own rendering" (p. 194).

518. ———. "The 'Romanticism' of Pope's Horace," *EIC,* X (1960), 390–404.

Explicates Pope's *Imitation of the First Satire of the Second Book of Horace,* stressing Pope's general alteration of Horace's "classically objective manner" to his own "Romantically subjective attitude . . ." (p. 392). Hunter concludes that Pope is "unHoratian" and that Pope's "Augustanism functioned in perspectives which have come to seem the exclusive property of the Romantic poets" (p. 404). See also entry 219.

519. Jack, Ian. "Pope and 'The Weighty Bullion of Dr. Donne's Satires,' " *PMLA,* LXVI (1951), 1009–22.

Examines Pope's debt to Donne on the basis of Pope's imitation of Donne's *Satire II* and *Satire IV.* Jack states that Pope most admired Donne's satiric imagery. See also 219.

520. Jones, Evan. "Verse, Prose and Pope: A Form of Sensibility," *MCR,* IV (1961), 30–40.

Provides an analysis of Pope's versification of John Donne's fourth satire. Jones states that Pope's couplets tend to degenerate into fragmented rhetoric which limits the range of his formal sensibility.

521. Levine, Jay Arnold. "Pope's *Epistle to Augustus,* Lines 1–30," *SEL,* VII (1967), 427–51.

Discusses the historical context, motifs, irony, and satire present in the exordium. Levine concludes that the "horror with which Pope viewed the antithesis of [his] kingly ideal in George II brought the *To Augustus* into being and dictated its mode of expression in the ironically conflated language of religion, politics, and poetry" (p. 451).

522. Maresca, Thomas E. "Pope's Defense of Satire: *The First Satire of the Second Book of Horace, Imitated,*" *ELH,* XXXI (1964), 366–94.

Examines and explicates in detail the literary theory and accomplishment of Pope's "satirist's apologia." Maresca concludes that "since it has been the whole purpose of the poem to prove that Pope does write true satire, the poem validates itself and proves its own argument" (p. 394).

523. ———. *Pope's Horatian Poems.* Columbus: Ohio State University Press, 1966.

Provides a study of Horatian satire as viewed by the eighteenth century; analyzes the influence of the traditional concept of Horace on Pope's *Imitations*; and explicates in depth the *First Satire of the Second Book of Horace, Epistle to Dr. Arbuthnot, Second Epistle of the Second Book of Horace,* and *First Epistle of the First Book of Horace.* In Appendix B, Maresca interprets two *Imitations* as "sermons on temperance" which employ "the structure of the Christian homily" (p. 211).

524. Midgley, E. G. "Pope, Suckling and Waller," *N&Q,* CXCV (1950), 386–87.

Maintains that lines 137–40 in the *Second Satire of the First Book of Horace* echo Waller's *A la Malade,* rather than any specific lines in Suckling.

525. Moskovit, Leonard Adolph. "Alexander Pope's *Imitations of Horace.*" Unpublished Ph.D. dissertation, University of California, Berkeley, 1963, *DA,* XXIV (1964), 5388—89.

Reading Pope's *Imitations* "as whole poems of a distinctive kind in the context of contemporary English attitudes," Moskovit studies the method and meaning of the *Imitations.*

526. Moskovit, Leonard Adolph. "Pope's Purposes in *Sober Advice*," *PQ*, XLIV (1965), 195–99.

Despite Pope's neglect of unity of theme, his use of translational rather than creative imitation, and his "rough humor on the subject of sex," Moskovit contends that the poem's notes contain "Pope's most thoughtful satire" (p. 198), and he concludes that Pope "blissfully" forgot "about his painfully created public persona in order to amuse himself, his close friends, and his readers" (p. 199) in *Sober Advice from Horace*.

527. Osborn, James M. "Pope, the Byzantine Empress, and Walpole's Whore," *RES*, n.s., VI (1955), 372–82.

Finds that the concluding passage of dialogue I of the *Epilogue to the Satires* contains a double allusion. The first allusion (initially noted by Warburton but subsequently disregarded) is to the marriage of the prostitute Theodora to Emperor Justinian in Procopius' *Secret History*, while the second allusion is to Robert Walpole's marriage to his mistress, Molly Skerrett. See also 219.

528. *Pittermann, Erwein. *Beobachtungen zum Vergleich von Popes "Imitations of Horace" mit ihrer Vorlage.* Manuscript Dissertation, Marburg, 1956.

529. Rawson, C. J. "Pope and Montaigne: A Parallel," *N&Q*, CCXI (1966), 459–60.

Notes an echo between lines 67–68 of Pope's *First Satire of the Second Book of Horace Imitated* and Montaigne's "Au Gibelin i' estois Guelphe. . . ."

530. Reichard, Hugo M. "The Drift of Pope's First *Epilogue*," *Boston University Studies in English*, IV (1960), 106–13.

Explicates the Triumph of Vice passage in dialogue I of Pope's *Epilogue to the Satires*. Reichard states that "Vice is so fashioned, by her rôle in the unifying plot of the poem, as to give an acute impression of modern society" (p. 106).

531. Ricks, Christopher. "A Debt of Pope to Swift," *N&Q*, CCIV (1959), 398–99.

Cites parallels between Swift's poem "Directions for a

Birth-day Song" and Pope's *First Epistle of the Second Book of Horace.*

532. Tillotson, Geoffrey. "Pope and Boileau," *N&Q,* CCV (1960), 294.

Suggests a parallel between the concluding line of Boileau's *Sixth Satire* and Pope's *First Epistle of the First Book of Horace.*

533. Williams, Aubrey L. "Pope and Horace: *The Second Epistle of the Second Book," Restoration and Eighteenth-Century Literature. Essays in Honor of Alan Dugald Mc-Killop.* Edited by Carroll Camden. Chicago: University of Chicago Press for William Marsh Rice University, 1963.

Explicates the epistle, placing emphasis on the new unity, focus, and design created by Pope's departures from the original. Williams demonstrates how Pope's controlling metaphor of thievery departs from (while it enhances) the metaphoric and thematic patterns of the original. See also 182.

534. *Zimmermann, Hans-Joachim. "Ein Autograph-Fragment von Popes *The Second Satire of Dr. John Donne, Versifyed,"* *Archiv,* CXCIX (1962), 173–81.

DUNCIAD

535. Bawcutt, N. W. "More Echoes in Pope's Poetry," *N&Q,*
ccIII (1958), 220–21.

Finds allusions to Shakespeare, Dryden, Lady Winchilsea,
and Prior in Pope's poetry, but especially in the *Dunciad.*

536. ———. "Pope's 'Duchesses and Lady Mary's': More Evidence," *N&Q,* ccvi (1961), 253–54.

Supports Aubrey L. Williams' argument (see 581) on
Dunciad, II, 123–32, by citing a passage from *Spectator,*
no. 205, as "the ultimate source" for the passage and for
A View of London and Westminster.

537. Berland, Alwyn. "Some Techniques of Fiction in Poetry,"
EIC, IV (1954), 372–85.

Contains an analysis of the fictional (as opposed to the
theatrical) structure of the *Dunciad* and *Epistle to Dr. Arbuthnot.*

538. Bloomfield, Morton W. "A Grammatical Approach to Personification Allegory," *MP,* LX (1963), 161–71.

Cites *Dunciad,* IV, 21–30, as an example of personification
allegory.

539. Bluestone, Max. "Pope's *Dunciad,* IV, 549," *Explicator,* XX
(1962), item 40.

Examines the culinary-religious ritual image in *Dunciad,*
IV, 549–62, and concludes that "Pope means that the amice
on the priest of culinary dulness has become an apron *engirdling* him as he performs his mystic rites."

540. Brooks, Benjamin Gilbert. "Pope's *Dunciad," Nineteenth
Century,* cxxxvII (1945), 135–41.

Reviews the Twickenham Edition of the *Dunciad,* edited
by James Sutherland (see 19), and provides a general interpretative study of the poem.

541. Chambers, Jessie Rhodes. "The Episode of Annius and Mummius: *Dunciad*, IV, 347–96," *PQ*, XLIII (1964), 185–92.

Explicates the historical, biblical, and allegorical aspects of the passage. Chambers concludes that the biblical images developed by Pope form "a continuous and coherent moral judgment" (p. 192) upon Mummius and Annius.

542. Chapin, Chester F. *Personification in Eighteenth-Century English Poetry*. New York: Columbia University Press, 1955.

In chapter six, Chapin briefly comments on Pope's theory of poetic imagination. Chapter seven contains an analysis of Pope's use of allegorical personification in the *Rape of the Lock* and *Dunciad*. Chapin focuses on the function of the allegorical figures (such as Dulness) as essential components of the structure of the *Dunciad*.

543. Crowther, John W., Jr. "Pope's Defense of Theology, Philosophy, and the Arts in *Dunciad*, IV," *Essays and Studies in English Literature*. Edited by Herbert H. Petit. Duquesne Studies—Philological Series, no. 5. Pittsburgh: Duquesne University Press, 1964.

Briefly comments on *Dunciad*, II, 459–83 and 643–50. See also 231.

544. Davison, J. A. "Bentley and the Greeks," *Proceedings of the Leeds Philosophical and Literary Society, Literary and Historical Section*, X (1963), 117–27.

States that although Bentley earned the enmity of Pope (in *Dunciad*, IV, for his criticism of Pope's Homer), "the main points [of his criticism] were points on which he was right and Pope was wrong."

545. Deneau, Daniel P. "Pope's 'Iv'ry Gate': *The Dunciad*, III, 340," *MLN*, LXXIV (1959), 208–11.

Cites the established tradition of the gates of ivory and horn and notes that, since the *Dunciad Variorum* (1729) concludes with the "Ivory Gate" allusion, the poem becomes more optimistic "than has been commonly realized" (p. 211). But since the 1743 version does not end with the allusion, Deneau suggests that the reference may be purposely ambiguous.

546. Dorris, George E. "Scipione Maffei Amid the Dunces," *RES*, n.s., XVI (1965), 288–90.

Provides the historical background of Maffei's acquaintance with Pope as a way of interpreting Pope's pseudo-scholarly note to *Dunciad*, IV, 201–2.

547. Edwards, Thomas Robert, Jr. "Light and Nature: A Reading of *The Dunciad*," *PQ*, XXXIX (1960), 447–63.

Provides a detailed analysis of the light-darkness and nature imagery in the *Dunciad* (1743). Edwards also discusses Pope's allusions, dramatic rhetoric, and theme. See also 219.

548. ———. "Pope's *Dunciad*, IV, 419–436," *Explicator*, XVI (1958), item 50.

States that the passage "is an extended parody of the ludicrous diction of bad pastoral poetry"; consequently, its satiric purpose explains Pope's use of circumlocution.

549. Erskine-Hill, Howard H. "The 'New World' of Pope's *Dunciad*," *Renaissance and Modern Studies*, VI (1962), 49–67.

Contrasts the action and subject matter of the *Rape of the Lock* and *Dunciad* in order to establish his contention that the latter is a deliberately different type of mock-heroic poem from the former and, therefore, should not be judged on the basis of the mock-heroic pattern observed in *Rape of the Lock*. Erskine-Hill examines the epic precedents and parallels in both poems; studies the element of fantasy in the *Dunciad*; and investigates the influence on the *Dunciad* of Erasmus' *In Praise of Folly*, Rabelais' *Gargantua and Pantagruel*, and Cervantes' *Don Quixote*. See also 219.

550. Fairclough, G. Thomas. "Pope and Boileau: A Supplementary Note," *Neuphilologische Mitteilungen*, LXIV (1963), 232–43.

Includes comparisons of brief passages from the *Dunciad* and other works of both Pope and Boileau. Fairclough asserts that "the object of satire (for either poet) is not literary or aesthetic, but moral or religious" (p. 233).

551. Friedman, Arthur. "Pope and Deism (*The Dunciad*, IV,

459–492)," *Pope and His Contemporaries: Essays Presented to George Sherburn.* Edited by James L. Clifford and Louis A. Landa. Oxford: Clarendon Press, 1949.

Explicates the passage in which Pope attempts to clarify his orthodoxy "by attacking the heterodoxies of others" (p. 89). Friedman concludes that the passage does suggest Pope's awareness "of the main issues involved in the deist controversy and that he was able to place himself on the side of orthodoxy . . ." (p. 95). See also 186.

552. Griffith, Reginald Harvey. "Pope's Reading," *N&Q*, CXCV (1950), 363–64.

Discusses an item in Pope's *Belesenheit* by commenting on the difference between the *Dunciad* of 1728 and the *Variorum* of 1729. Griffith states that Pope was busy from April of 1729 through the summer in collecting adverse criticism against him such as Edmund Curll's *Curliad*.

553. ———. *"The Dunciad,"* PQ, XXIV (1945), 155–57.

Quotes a couplet from *Essay on Criticism* (II, 264–65) as a basis for his contention that *"The Dunciad* is not a digression . . ."* but "continues the doctrine of the *Essay on Criticism."* See also 219.

554. Hauser, David R. "Medea's Strain and Hermes' Wand: Pope's Use of Mythology," *MLN*, LXXVI (1961), 224–29.

Examines Pope's mythological allusions in *Dunciad*, IV, 635–40.

555. Hopkins, Robert H. " 'The good old cause' in Pope, Addison, and Steele," *RES*, n.s., XVII (1966), 62–68.

Traces the genesis of "good old cause" and interprets Pope's varied uses of the phrase in *Dunciad*, V, 81; *Dunciad*, I, 205; *First Epistle of the First Book of Horace Imitated*, 98; Epistle III, 189.

556. Johnson, Carol Holmes. "Pope's *Dunciad*: Requisitions of Verity," *Southern Review*, n.s., I (Winter-Spring, 1965), 108–16.

States that Pope's *Dunciad* contains " 'reason reasoned' rather than reasoning" (p. 108) in that "the rightness of his premises appears self-evident, even discounting the necessarily rigged nature of the contest in which Pope had to invent both the opposition and the defense and in doing so arranged for the opposition's own disclosures to be self-condemning" (p. 115). See also 557.

557. Johnson, Carol Holmes. *Reason's Double Agents.* Chapel Hill: University of North Carolina Press, 1966.

In the chapter entitled "Alexander Pope: Requisitions of Verity," Johnson discusses Pope's use of language and logic in the *Dunciad.* See also 556.

558. Kenner, Hugh. *Gnomon: Essays on Contemporary Literature.* New York: McDowell, Obolensky, 1958.

Cites passages from the *Dunciad* and briefly comments on Pope's poetic sensibility and his concept of "Universal Darkness."

559. Kernan, Alvin B. "*The Dunciad* and the Plot of Satire," *SEL,* II (1962), 255–66.

Provides a detailed analysis of the "expansion-contraction pattern" and the ironic patterns of movement in the *Dunciad.* Kernan concludes that "the spread of dulness is a contraction of life. This would seem to be the central irony . . . and action which the plot imitates on many levels" (p. 266). See also 219.

560. Leavis, F. R. *The Common Pursuit.* London: Chatto & Windus, 1952.

Briefly examines *Dunciad,* IV. Leavis describes book IV as "a self-sufficient poem" (p. 91) and studies Pope's concept of "order."

561. Marshall, Robert Carlisle. "Aesthetic Aspects of Pope's *Dunciad*: A Critical Study." Unpublished Ph.D. dissertation, University of Texas, 1963, *DA,* XXIV (1964), 2909–10.

In studying the "artistic techniques" of the construction and unification of the *Dunciad,* Marshall examines the prosody, imagery, and the "syntactical, figurative, and tonal patterns which function in the aesthetic operation of the poem."

562. Maxwell, J. C. *"Dunciad,* IV, 121–122," *RES,* n.s., III (1952), 55.

> States that the Pope-Warburton note in reference to lines 121–22 is from Ovid's *Metamorphoses,* vii, 170 and 292.

563. ———. "Look . . . What!: A Late Instance," *N&Q,* CCVII (1962), 19.

> Cites a 1743 instance of the word *look* followed by an interrogative pronoun in Pope's "Ricardus Aristarchus of the Hero of the Poem," prefixed to *Dunciad,* IV. Maxwell suggests that this usage may be a deliberate archaism on Pope's part."

564. Moore, John Robert. "Gildon's Attack on Steele and Defoe in *The Battle of the Authors,*" *PMLA,* LXVI (1951), 534–38.

> Suggests that Pope may have utilized Charles Gildon's *Battle of the Authors* as a source for the *Dunciad.*

565. Peavy, Charles Druery, III. "Cibber's Crown of Dulness: A Re-examination of the Pope–Cibber Controversy." Unpublished Ph.D. dissertation, Tulane University, 1963, *DA,* XXV (1964), 454.

> Examines "the history and progress of Pope's feud with Cibber" and studies the "allegorical, moral, and anagogical implications of the 1743 *Dunciad."* Peavy concludes that Cibber's enthronement was not caused by Cibber's allusion to Pope in *The Rehearsal* but by Cibber's lack of aesthetic and moral values.

566. *Pinkus, Philip. "Pope, Cibber, and the Crown of Dulness," *South Central Bulletin,* vol. XXVI, no. 4 (1966; pub. 1967), pp. 17–27.

567. ———. "Satire and St. George," *QQ,* LXX (1963), 30–49.

> Lists Pope's *Dunciad* and *Rape of the Lock* as examples of satire based on the triumph of the dragon of literary evil over St. George.

568. Potts, Abbie Findlay. "The Case for Internal Evidence

(7) : Butterflies and Butterfly-Hunters," *BNYPL*, LXIII (1959), 148–52.

On the basis of internal evidence, Potts finds that Shakespeare's description of a butterfly and butterfly-hunter in *Coriolanus* (I, iii, 62–71) is echoed in the *Dunciad* (IV, 421–36) and in Wordsworth's stanzas "To a Butterfly."

569. Reichard, Hugo M. "Pope's Social Satire: Belles-Lettres and Business," *PMLA*, LXVII (1952), 420–34.

Examines Pope's treatment of and the function of the commercialized man of letters and those groups who are responsible for the degradation of literature and the chaotic movement of "the Smithfield Muses to the Ear of Kings." See also 219.

570. Rogers, Robert W. *The Major Satires of Alexander Pope.* Illinois Studies in Language and Literature, vol. XL. Urbana : University of Illinois Press, 1955.

States that Pope was motivated to write satirical verse because of intense literary and personal criticism; investigates the inception, composition, and publication of the *Dunciad Variorum, Essay on Man, Moral Essays,* and *Imitations of Horace*; and determines that they reflect Pope's growth as a satirist and represent changes in Pope's interests.

Reviewed by John Butt, *PQ*, XXXV (1956), 321–22; *TLS*, December 30, 1955, p. 792; Clarence Tracy, *QQ*, LXIII (1957), 459; A. R. Humphreys, *MLR*, LII (1957), 260–61; Geoffrey Tillotson, *MP*, LV (1957), 61–62; Aubrey L. Williams, *MLN*, LXXII (1957), 221–22; Norman Callan, *RES*, n.s., IX (1958), 214–16; James R. Sutherland, *JEGP*, LVII (1958), 345–46.

571. Sambrook, A. J. "A Possible Source of 'Master of the Sev'nfold Face' in *The Dunciad* (B)," *N&Q*, XIV (1967), 409–10.

Cites the *Scribleriad* (London, 1742), where the phrase occurs.

572. Sherbo, Arthur. "Pope and Boileau," *N&Q*, CXCVI (1951), 495.

Comments that Joseph Warton, in his *Essay on the*

Genius and Writings of Pope, compared a line from Boileau's first satire with *Dunciad,* I, 295, but that editions of the *Dunciad* do not mention this apparent borrowing or imitation.

573. Sherburn, George. *"The Dunciad,* Book IV," *Essential Articles for the Study of Alexander Pope.* Edited by Maynard Mack. Hamden, Conn.: Shoestring Press, 1964.

Examines the "intellectual content" of lines 138–336 and 459–516; contends that the structure and individual episodes of Henry Fielding's farcical plays furnished a model for the structure of *Dunciad,* IV; and studies the variety of imagery in the poem. Also published in *TSLL,* XXIV (1944), 174–90.

574. Smith, Constance I. "An Echo of Dryden in Pope," *N&Q,* CCX (1965), 451.

Cites a parallel between *Dunciad,* III, 356, and Dryden's sixth book of Homer's *Iliad,* 116–17.

575. Stiker, J. M. " 'Bladen' and 'Hays': Pope's *Dunciad,* IV, 560," *N&Q,* CCXI (1966), 458–59.

Identifies Martin Bladen and Charles Hays, thus providing an allusion by Pope to the slave trade.

576. Sutherland, James R. " 'The Dull Duty of an Editor,' " *RES,* XXI (1945), 202–15.

Explains the opposing views on editorial commentary held by Theobald and Pope. Sutherland also interprets the critical prose commentary of the *Dunciad* as not only an attack on editing, verbal criticism, textual critics, Theobald, and *Shakespeare Restored,* but also as a significant component of Pope's satirical intention. See also 219.

577. Tanner, Tony. "Reason and the Grotesque: Pope's *Dunciad,*" *CritQ,* VII (1965), 145–60.

Interprets grotesque as "an attempt to invoke and subdue the demonic aspects of the world" (p. 159). Tanner contends that Pope successfully made this attempt in the *Dunciad* by employing "paradoxical pessimism" as the "extreme ironic disjunction between form and content" (p. 146) in the *Dunciad.*

578. Vieth, David M. "Pope's *Dunciad,* I, 203–204, and Christ among the Elders," *PLL,* II (Winter, 1966), 71–73.

   The biblical allusion "chair'd . . . amidst the Doctors" is part of the organization of book I, which "recapitulates, in chronological sequence, some of the main events of biblical history from the Creation to the baptism of Christ."

579. ———. "Pope's *Dunciad,* IV, 403–419," *Explicator,* XXV (1966), item 36.

   Sees the carnation grower "satirized in terms resembling the popular conception of Victorian melodrama."

580. Williams, Aubrey L. "Literary Backgrounds to Book Four of *The Dunciad,*" *PMLA,* LXVIII (1953), 806–13.

   Examines two sources for the "theatrical coloration" in *Dunciad,* IV; the *Tablet of Cebes* and *Advices From Parnassus,* a 1727 translation of Boccalini's *Ragguagli di Parnaso.*

581. ———. "Pope's 'Duchesses and Lady Mary's,' " *RES,* n.s., IV (1953), 359–61.

   Disagrees with Sutherland's interpretation (see 19) of *Dunciad,* II, 123–32. Williams cites Pope's annotation to the passage and the anonymous *A View of London and Westminster* to support his contention that the meaning of the lines were public and not just personal as Sutherland had suggested. See also 536.

582. ———. *Pope's Dunciad: A Study of Its Meaning.* Baton Rouge: Louisiana State University Press, 1955.

   This critical and interpretative study is based on the four major editions of the *Dunciad* in order to "reveal a progressive expansion of the poem's meaning and imaginative range" (p. vii). Williams focuses on the problems peculiar to each of the four editions and discusses the historical, ethical, philosophical, and stylistic aspects of each edition. Chapter six, "The Anti-Christ of Wit," is a comparative study of the influence of Milton's *Paradise Lost* on the *Dunciad.*

   Reviewed by Curt A. Zimansky, *PQ,* XXXV (1956), 322–23; *TLS,* December 30, 1955, p. 792; Donald Davie, *EIC,*

VI (1956), 319–25; Bruce Dearing, *CE*, XVII (1955), 421; Louis I. Bredvold, *MP*, LIV (1956), 280–81; Robert W. Rogers, *JEGP*, LVI (1957), 146–48; Rachel Trickett, *RES*, n.s., VIII (1957), 316–19; Ernest Tuveson, *MLN*, LXXII (1957), 542–46; Hugh Kenner, *Poetry*, LXXXVIII (1956), 277–81.

OTHER WRITINGS

583. Boddy, Margaret. "Tonson's 'Loss of Rowe,'" *N&Q*, CCXI (1966), 213–14.

> Interprets a line ("Lintot, farewell! thy bard must go") from Pope's "Farewell to London."

584. Boyce, Benjamin. "An Annotated Volume from Pope's Library," *N&Q*, CCIII (1958), 55–57.

> Comments on Pope's annotations found within his personal copy of *A New Collection of Poems Relating to State Affairs* and suggests Pope's authorship of the third stanza of a poem by Dorset and a poem entitled "On the Death of the Queen and Marshal Luxembourg." See also 585, 587, and 612.

585. Cameron, W. J. "Pope's Annotations on 'State Affairs' Poems," *N&Q*, CCIII (1958), 291–94.

> Criticizes Benjamin Boyce's article (see 584) by contending that Pope's reading of *A New Collection of Poems Relating to State Affairs* was cursory; that his annotations were not extensive, but do reveal varied interests; that Pope's authorship of the third stanza of Dorset's poem "may be dismissed"; and that his authorship of "On the Death of the Queen and Marshal Luxembourg" is highly unlikely.

586. Cawley, A. C. "Chaucer, Pope, and Fame," *REL*, III (April, 1962), 9–19.

> Examines the significance of Chaucer's and Pope's uses of and attitudes toward fame by comparing Pope's *Temple of Fame* with Chaucer's *House of Fame*.

587. Chapple, J. A. V. "Dorset on Dorchester," *N&Q*, CCIII (1958), 294.

> Disagrees with Benjamin Boyce (see 584) by disclaiming Pope's authorship of the third stanza of Dorset's poem.

588. Douglas, Loyd. " 'A severe animadversion on Bossu,' " *PMLA*, LXII (1947), 690–706.

Maintains that, despite Joseph Warton's misinterpretative footnote to chapter fifteen of *Peri Bathous* ("A Receipt to Make an Epic Poem"), Pope did not depreciate René Le Bossu. On the basis of *Guardian*, no. 78 (where the "Receipt" originally appeared), Douglas asserts that Pope admired Le Bossu and was primarily ridiculing Sir Richard Blackmore and other English disciples of Le Bossu.

589. Erskine-Hill, Howard H. "Alexander Pope at Fifteen: A New Manuscript," *RES*, n.s., XVII (1966), 268–77.

Discovered among the Caryll papers in the British Museum, versions of Pope's "The River" and "Upon Silence" and an hitherto unknown eighteen-line poem dated 1703, "On Some Flowers in Silk Wrought by a Handsome Young Lady." Erskine-Hill also discusses Pope's early friendship with Caryll.

590. Fineman, Daniel A. "The Motivation of Pope's *Guardian* 40," *MLN*, LXVII (1952), 24–28.

Finds that an implicit reference in *Guardian*, no. 30, to Pope's translation of Chaucer's *Merchant's Tale* as an example of Pope's pastorals provoked Pope to write his ironical reply in *Guardian*, no. 40.

591. Fuller, John. "A New Epilogue by Pope?" *RES*, n.s., XVII (1966), 409–13.

Substantiates through internal and historical evidence his contention that Pope wrote the "Epilogue" to John Gay's "quasi-Chaucerian comedy," *The Wife of Bath*.

592. Gillie, Christopher. "Alexander Pope: 'Elegy to the Memory of an Unfortunate Lady,'" *Interpretations*. Edited by John Wain. London: Routledge & Kegan Paul, 1955.

Reprints the text of the elegy and explicates the poem on the basis of its ethical attitude, theme, and diction.

593. Hopkins, Robert H. "The John Dunton-Steele (?) Yoking in Pope's 'Sandys's Ghost,'" *N&Q*, CCIX (1964), 53–55.

Contends that line 52 of Pope's "Sandys's Ghost" refers to Richard Steele.

594. Hunting, Robert S. "The 'Cura Cuiusdam Anonymi' of Pope's *Anthologia*," *PQ*, XXXI (1952), 430–32.

Questions the validity of the 1684 ascription of *Anthologia* to Francis Atterbury, because Pope in the title page of his 1740 enlargement of the 1684 edition indicated that the original author was unknown to him. Hunting asserts that, since Pope and Atterbury were friends, it was unlikely that Pope would not have known the work of Atterbury; consequently, Hunting advances the name of Thomas Power as a more probable candidate (see 609).

595. Kerby-Miller, Charles (ed.). *Memoirs of the Extraordinary Life, Works, and Discoveries of Martinus Scriblerus.* New Haven: Yale University Press, 1950.

In his preface, Kerby-Miller provides an extensive examination of the Scriblerus Club and the authorship, composition, publication, and literary background of the *Memoirs*. The preface also includes a bibliography of major editions published from 1741 to 1932. A reproduction of the text of the *Memoirs* is followed by notes to each chapter of the text and by six appendices. See also 596.

Reviewed by Donald Cornu, *MLQ*, XI (1950), 502–4; Herbert Davis, *PQ*, XXX (1951), 254–56; William Henry Irving, *SAQ*, L (1951), 152–53; Richmond P. Bond, *MLR*, XLVII (1952), 67; Maurice Johnson, *MLN*, LXVII (1952), 571–73; Robert W. Rogers, *JEGP*, LI (1952), 107–8; Paul Turner, *ES*, XXXIII (1952), 224–26; John Butt, *RES*, n.s., IV (1953), 91.

596. McKillop, Alan Dugald. "The Geographical Chapter in *Scriblerus*," *MLN*, LXVIII (1953), 480–81.

Disagrees with Charles Kerby-Miller (see 595). McKillop states that the source for the geographical passage in the *Memoirs of Martinus Scriblerus* is Bernhardus Varenius' *Geographia Generalis.*

597. Maud, Ralph N. "Pope and Miss Betty Marriot," *MLN*, LXXII (1957), 96–97.

Agrees with Norman Ault (see 165) that Pope's *Coronation Epistle* was addressed to Teresa Blount, but suggests that the poem was inspired by Betty Marriot, a young girl "by whom Pope was undoubtedly captivated" (p. 96).

598. Maud, Ralph N. "Some Lines from Pope," *RES*, n.s., IX (1958), 146–51.

Explicates sixteen lines which have been regarded as the suppressed conclusion to the *Coronation Epistle* (Twickenham Edition, VI, *Minor Poems*). Maud asserts that the lines are a "genuine Pope fragment," but that their "incompatibility" with the poem suggests the probability that the lines have been "mistakenly assigned." See also 604.

599. Maxwell, J. C. "Pope's Statius and Dryden's Ovid," *N&Q*, CCIX (1964), 56.

Notes a parallel between lines 5–6 of Pope's translation of the *Thebaid*, I, and Dryden's translation of lines 5–6 of the *Metamorphoses*, I.

600. Mead, G. C. F. "A Pope Inscription," *TLS*, October 7, 1949, p. 649.

Describes and quotes an unpublished inscription by Pope found on the west side of a monument erected to the memory of John Oliver in 1741.

601. Mell, Donald Charles, Jr. "Variations on Elegiac Themes: Dryden, Pope, Prior, Gray, Johnson." Unpublished Ph.D. dissertation, University of Pennsylvania, 1961, *DA*, XXII (1961), 1159–60.

Examines Pope's "Elegy to the Memory of an Unfortunate Lady" and discusses the varied ways Pope responded "to the paradoxical aspects of morality." Mell concludes that "the unity of the 'Elegy' is in its variety" (p. 1159).

602. Mudrick, Marvin. "Chaucer as Librettist," *PQ*, XXXVIII (1959), 21–29.

Cites excerpts from Pope's "modernization" or "imitation" of Chaucer's "Prologue to The Wife of Bath's Tale" and *Merchant's Tale* and concludes that Pope, like Dryden, tried to adapt Chaucer to the Augustan "idiom . . . of different, simpler and more formal values" (p. 29).

603. Rogers, Robert W. "Alexander Pope's *Universal Prayer*," *JEGP*, LIV (1955), 612–24.

Prints "four transcripts which purport to be based on

authoritative manuscripts" (p. 612) of the *Universal Prayer*. Rogers compares the texts, focusing on major aspects of the poem which remained constant and on emendations. See also 219.

604. Ryley, Robert Michael. "A Note on the Authenticity of Some Lines from Pope," *PQ*, XLVI (1967), 417–21.

Argues against Maud's theory (see entry 598) that the suppressed sixteen lines of the *Coronation Epistle* are "part of another poem now lost" (p. 417), explains external and internal evidence, and concludes that the "tentative and experimental" lines are part of the *Coronation Epistle*.

605. Sackett, S. J. "Neoclassical Tendencies," *Fort Hays Studies*. Literature Series, no. 1, June, 1962, pp. xiii-xviii.

Provides an introductory explanation of Pope's method and design in the *Art of Sinking in Poetry*. Sackett emphasizes the significance of *Peri Bathous* on the basis of what it reveals about Pope's standards and attitude toward poetry.

606. Seamon, Roger G. "The Rhetorical Pattern of Mock-Heroic Satire," *The Humanities Association Bulletin*, vol. XVII, no. 2 (1966), pp. 37–41.

Sees the "nature of mock-heroic satire" as a process which "moves from the comic to the novelistic perspective." Seamon illustrates his point by quoting a brief passage from *Peri Bathous*.

607. Sherburn, George. "The 'Copies of Verses' about *Gulliver*," *TSLL*, III (1961), 3–7.

Suggests that the five commendatory verses "generally ascribed *in toto* to Pope" (p. 3) were "the result of typical Scriblerian collaboration" (p. 7).

608. Shugrue, Michael. "Pope's Translation of Statius," *N&Q*, CCII (1957), 463.

Determines that Pope translated the *First Book of the Thebais* by Statius because Pope came to admire and respect Statius' work through his association with his first tutor, Banister, a priest.

609. Sparrow, John. "Pope's *Anthologia* Again," *PQ*, XXXIII (1954), 428–31.

Disagrees with Robert S. Hunting (see 594). Sparrow claims that *anonymous* means "un-named" and that Pope knew that the anonymous editor was Atterbury but respected the latter's wish for anonymity.

610. Steeves, Edna Leake (ed.). *The Art of Sinking in Poetry: Martinus Scriblerus'* ΠΕΡΙ ΒΑΘΟΤΣ: *A Critical Edition.* With bibliographical notes on "the last volume" of the Swift-Pope *Miscellanies* by Reginald Harvey Griffith and E. L. Steeves. New York: Columbia University, 1952.

Reproduces the text of *Peri Bathous* and includes an extensive commentary with notes "arranged by chapter with page and line references to the text" (p. 96). Steeves' critical-interpretative introduction examines the history, composition, authorship, and publication of *Peri Bathous* and analyzes the literary background, satire, and poetical theory of the work.

Reviewed by Benjamin Boyce, *SAQ*, LI (1952), 619; Charles Kerby-Miller, *PQ*, XXXII (1953), 286–88; Robert W. Rogers, *JEGP*, LII (1953), 422–23; Earl R. Wasserman, *MLN*, LXVIII (1953), 436–37.

611. Surtz, Edward L. "Epithets in Pope's *Messiah*," *PQ*, XXVII (1948), 209–18.

Notes adverse criticism of the *Messiah*, describes the traditional and current use of epithets in the eighteenth century, and examines the extent to which Pope applied four classes of epithets in the *Messiah*. Surtz concludes that the poem is a "defective success" because Pope's epithets are too redundant.

612. Tillotson, Geoffrey. "Pope and an Anonymous Epitaph," *N&Q*, CCIII (1958), 437–38.

Substantiates Benjamin Boyce's contention (see 584) that Pope was the author of the epitaph "On the Death of the Queen and Marshal Luxembourg."

613. ———. "Pope's *Epistle to Harley*: An Analysis," *Pope and His Contemporaries: Essays Presented to George Sher-*

burn. Edited by James L. Clifford and Louis A. Landa. Oxford: Clarendon Press, 1949.

Reprints the text and explicates the epistle (written for the memory of Parnell and dedicated to Harley) on the basis of the Parnell-Pope-Harley relationship, the poem's diction, and its typography. See also 186.

614. Torchiana, Donald T. "Brutus: Pope's Last Hero," *JEGP*, LXI (1962), 853–67.

Describes Pope's epic plan for *Brutus*; suggests that the plan was influenced by the Patriot Opposition and specifically Pope's political friendship with Lyttelton; examines the "ethical and philosophical independence" (p. 859) of the plan which is closely linked with epistle III of *Essay on Man*; and considers the career of Brutus as a positive "corrective" to the political and ecclesiastical abuses depicted in *Dunciad*, IV.

615. Vieth, David M. "Pope and Rochester: An Unnoticed Borrowing," *N&Q*, CCXI (1966), 457–58.

Interprets a line from Pope's *Prologue, Design'd for Mr. Durfy's Last Play* which was borrowed from the earl of Rochester's *An Epistolary from M.G. to O.B. upon Their Mutual Poems*.

616. Wasserman, Earl R. "Pope's *Ode for Musick*," *ELH*, XXVIII (1961), 163–86.

Contains a brief analysis of Dryden's "Song for St. Cecilia's Day" and a detailed explication of Pope's *Ode for Musick. On St. Cecilia's Day*. Wasserman focuses on the diction, theme, symbolism, and structural complexity of Pope's ode. See also 219.

617. *Zimmermann, Hans-Joachim. "Bemerkungen zum Manuskript und Text von Popes *Brutus*," *Archiv*, CXCIX (1962), 100–106.

POPE AS A TRANSLATOR AND EDITOR

618. Boyce, Benjamin. "Pope's Yews in Shakespeare's Grave-yard," *N&Q*, CXCIX (1954), 287.

> Maintains that future editors of Shakespeare's *Romeo and Juliet* should not include Pope's "bold alterations" of "yew-trees" for Shakespeare's "young trees."

619. Callan, Norman. "Pope's *Iliad*: A New Document," *RES*, n.s., IV (1953), 109–21.

> Contains an analysis of the Bibliothèque de l'Arsenal's "collection of the proofsheets of the first eight books of Pope's *Iliad*, bound as a single volume [see 642] and corrected by Pope himself" (p. 109). Callan concludes as follows: the numerous corrections either rectify printer's errors or contain Pope's revisions of a single word or of an entire passage; since author revisions occur only in books IV through VIII, Pope's intention to publish his translation before Tickell's was genuine; Pope's "knowledge of Greek is in his favour" (p. 118). See also 219.
>
> Reviewed by Douglas Knight, *PQ*, XXXIII (1954), 289–90.

620. Clark, David Ridgley. "Landscape Painting Effects in Pope's Homer," *Journal of Aesthetics and Art Criticism*, XXII (1963), 25–28.

> Discusses Pope's "understanding of recent and contemporary landscape painting" in relationship to his concept of Homer and the classical epic.

621. Clarke, Martin L. *Greek Studies in England, 1700–1830*. Cambridge: At the University Press, 1945.

> In his chapter entitled "Greek Poetry: Homer," Clarke briefly considers Pope's translation of Homer. Clarke states that although Pope "misrepresented" Homer, he did have a true appreciation for Homer, and that "many" of Pope's critical comments in his preface and notes "are just and valuable" (p. 125).

622. Cronin, Grover, Jr., and Doyle, Paul A. (eds.). *Pope's*

Iliad: An Examination by William Melmoth. Washington: Catholic University of America Press, 1960.

Provides three critical essays on Pope's *Iliad* by William "Pliny" Melmoth, and variant readings of nine separate editions.

Reviewed by Irvin Ehrenpreis, *Classical Journal,* LVI (1960), 42; C. J. Rawson, *N&Q,* CCVI (1961), 439–40; Hans-Joachim Zimmermann, *Archiv,* CXCIX (1962), 52–55.

623. Dixon, Peter. "Edward Bysshe and Pope's Shakespeare," *N&Q,* CCIX (1964), 292–93.

Suggests that "Pope's taste in Shakespeare" may have been influenced by Edward Bysshe's *Art of English Poetry.*

624. ———. "Pope's Shakespeare," *JEGP,* LXIII (1964), 191–203.

In an attempt to discover what Pope most admired in Shakespeare, Dixon examines Pope's debt to other neoclassic critics. Dixon concludes that Pope had a "strong editorial preference . . . for Shakespeare, the satirist" (p. 191).

625. *Donaghey, Brian S. "Alexander Pope's and Sir William Trumbull's Translations of Boethius," *Leeds Slovenski Etnograf,* I (1967), 71–82.

626. *Fabian, Bernhard. "Pope und die goldene Kette Homers," *Anglia,* LXXXII (1964), 150–71.

627. *Frost, William. "Ulysses, Diomed and Dolon: Pope and the Predecessors," *Lebende Antike: Symposion für Rudolf Sühnel.* Edited by Horst Meller and Hans-Joachim Zimmermann. Berlin: E. Schmidt, 1967.

628. Goldstein, Malcolm. "Pope, Sheffield, and Shakespeare's *Julius Caesar,*" *MLN,* LXXI (1956), 8–10.

States that, since Pope was editing (from 1721 to 1724) both the collected works of John Sheffield and the plays of Shakespeare, his editorial judgment in regard to "his emendations of Shakespeare's *Julius Caesar*" (p. 8) was influenced "by turns of phrase and alternations in Shakespeare's text" (p. 8) found in Sheffield's *Tragedy of Julius Caesar.*

629. Gustafson, Richard Clarence. "The Perspicuous and the Sublime: A Historical Study of the Language of Pope's *Iliad*." Unpublished Ph.D. dissertation, University of Kansas, 1960, *DA*, XXI (1961), 2703–4.

Examines Pope's use of rhetoric, inversions, and native and classical grammar and finds that Pope introduced moral issues not found in Homer, organized Homer's speeches in the structure of Renaissance rhetoric, allegorized characters, and exalted his language rather than concern himself with literal fidelity.

630. Hussey, Richard. "A Note on Pope's Homer, III: The Free Fantasias," *N&Q*, CLXXXVIII (1945), 10–11.

Suggests that Pope's habit of straying from his text and straining grammar for rime may be termed "a free fantasia on the theme" (p. 10).

631. ———. "A Note on Pope's Homer, IV: Absurdities," *N&Q*, CLXXXVIII (1945), 24–28.

Lists twenty-six "absurdities" or examples of inept or deliberately distorted translations; cites Pope's exaggerated use of certain words or phrases; states that since Pope's knowledge of Greek was limited, he plagiarized from Chapman, Ogilby, and Madame Dacier; and takes issue with Pope's use of colloquial contractions and corroborative detail.

632. ———. "A Note on Pope's Homer, V: Epithets Expanded," *N&Q*, CLXXXVIII (1945), 49–52.

Cites examples of Pope's expanded epithets, errors in translation, exaggeration, "lingo," generalizations, and misuse of numbers.

633. ———. "A Note on Pope's Homer, VI: Factitious Vigour," *N&Q*, CLXXXVIII (1945), 74–76.

Provides examples of Pope's exaggerated diction and pathos.

634. Knight, Douglas. "The Development of Pope's *Iliad* Preface: A Study of the Manuscript," *MLQ*, XVI (1955), 237–46.

Examines the stages of development in the prose Preface

to *Iliad* by investigating Pope's revisions and modifications. Knight concludes that in the finished preface, "Pope creates . . . a speaking voice which is both interpretative and oracular; this voice describes Homer's greatness with individual vigor but in stylistic terms which place it beyond the range of mere individual opinion" (p. 246). See also 219.

635. Knight, Douglas. "Homer's Translators," *TLS*, May 4, 1946, p. 211.

Disagrees with H. L. Lorimer (see 638) and states that Pope was familiar with Eustathius and able to translate his notes.

636. ———. *Pope and the Heroic Tradition: A Critical Study of His Iliad.* New Haven: Yale University Press, 1951.

In chapter one, Knight examines the nature and assumptions underlying the adverse criticism of Pope's translation of the *Iliad*; emphasizes Pope's conscious awareness of Homer's poetic power and "epicness"; and studies Pope's attitude toward the responsibilities and problems of a translator. In his second chapter, Knight provides an extensive analysis of Pope's style in relationship to Homer's style and meaning. Knight's basic conclusion is that Pope's skill in combining the heroic tradition with the contemporary produced an effective variety which was appropriate to the epic tradition and to Homer's heroic poetry.

Reviewed by Clarence Tracy, *QQ*, LIX (1953), 408–9; Norman Callan, *PQ*, XXXI (1952), 289–90; H. C. Fay, *RES*, n.s., IV (1953), 291–92; H. T. Swedenberg, *MLN*, LXVIII (1953), 432–33.

637. ———. "Pope as a Student of Homer," *CL*, IV (1952), 75–82.

Knight analyzes Pope's position as a translator of Homer; states that Pope accepted the heroic tradition but interpreted Homer "within a context that concedes historical change" (p. 75); and concludes that, for Pope, Homer was "a primary means of maintaining ordered values in poetry and criticism" (p. 82).

638. Lorimer, H. L. "Homer and Pope," *TLS*, March 9, 1946, p. 115.

Argues that Pope relied on Madame Dacier's notes for

his translation of the *Iliad* and suggests that Pope was not familiar with Eustathius (see 635).

639. McAleer, John J. "Alexander Pope—Shakespeare's Second Editor," *Shakespeare Newsletter,* XVI (1966), 32.

Provides a biographical account of Pope's relationship to his edition of Shakespeare.

640. Rousseau, G. S. "Seven Types of *Iliad,*" *English Miscellany,* XVI (1965), 143–67.

Studies *Iliad,* VIII, 553–65, in the hands of seven translators, including Pope.

641. Ryskamp, Charles. " 'Epigrams I More Especially Delight In': The Receipts for Pope's *Iliad,*" *Princeton University Library Chronicle,* XXIV (1962), 36–38.

Provides an illustration of two receipts for Pope's *Iliad* which are not dated but are signed by Pope. Ryskamp quotes a letter from Pope to John Caryll in which Pope calls the receipts "epigrams."

642. Schmitz, Robert M. "The 'Arsenal' Proof Sheets of Pope's *Iliad*: A Third Report," *MLN,* LXXIV (1959), 486–89.

Challenges the findings of Norman Callan (see 619) regarding "a bound volume of proof sheets for Books I-VIII of Pope's *Iliad*" (p. 486). Schmitz maintains that the "Arsenal" volume is not in one piece and that there were four issues of Pope's *Iliad* during the period June 6, 1715, to March 22, 1716. See also 219.

643. Sen, Sailendra Kumar. "Shakespeare as a Borrower: Kellet and Eighteenth-Century Critics," *N&Q,* CCVIII (1963), 332–34.

Provides a quote in which Pope discusses Shakespeare's practice of omitting or not clarifying details in the plots of his plays.

644. Smith, David Nichol (ed.). *Eighteenth Century Essays on Shakespeare.* 2d ed. Oxford: Clarendon Press, 1963.

Provides the text of Pope's Preface to *Shakespeare* (1725).

645. *Sühnel, Rudolf. *Homer und die englische Humanität; Chapmans und Popes Übersetzungskunst im Rahmen der humanistischen Tradition.* Tübingen: M. Niemeyer, 1958.

Reviewed by Bernhard Fabian, *Archiv,* CXCVI (1960), 350–51; Edgar Lohner, *JEGP,* LIX (1960), 735–37; C. H. Salter, *RES,* n.s., XI (1960), 85–86; William Frost, *PQ,* XXXVIII (1959), 342–43.

646. *Zimmermann, Hans-Joachim. "Alexander Pope und die homerischen Fliegen: Ein Beitrag zur philologischen Entomologie," *Lebende Antike: Symposion für Rudolf Sühnel.* Edited by Horst Meller and Hans-Joachim Zimmermann. Berlin: E. Schmidt, 1967.

647. ———. *Alexander Popes Noten zu Homer: Eine Manuskript- und Quellenstudie.* Studien zum Fortwirken der Antike, 2. Heidelberg, 1966.

CORRESPONDENCE

648. Arlidge, Elizabeth. "A New Pope Letter," *RES*, n.s., XII (1961), 398–402.

Transcribes the text of a "previously unpublished letter from Pope to William Broome . . . written during the period of Pope's work on the *Iliad*" (p. 398) and briefly comments on Broome's relationship with Pope and Young.

649. Bond, Donald F. "The Importance of Pope's Letters," *MP*, LVI (1958), 55–59.

Reviews *The Correspondence of Alexander Pope*, edited by George Sherburn (see 670). Bond includes a list of corrections that "should be made in a second edition" (p. 57). See also 219.

650. Burgess, C. F. "Mr. Gay, Amanuensis," *N&Q*, CCIX (1964), 293.

Identifies a Pope letter which was sent to Edward Harley as written by John Gay but dictated by Pope.

651. Butt, John. "Pope Seen Through His Letters," *Eighteenth-Century English Literature: Modern Essays in Criticism*. Edited by James L. Clifford. New York: Oxford University Press, 1959.

Presents a brief account of Pope's publishing intrigues with respect to his correspondence and suggests that Pope's letters are a record of the poet's friendships. This essay first appeared under the title "Alexander Pope: A New View of His Character" in *Listener*, LVII (June 20, 1957), 999, 1003. See also 185.

652. ———. "Pope's Letters: Some Notes and Corrections," *N&Q*, CCII (1957), 463–66.

Corrects, annotates, or interprets twelve points in George Sherburn's edition of Pope's correspondence (see 670).

653. Cowler, Rosemary Elizabeth. "Shadow and Substance: A Discussion of Pope's Correspondence," *The Familiar Let-*

ter in the Eighteenth Century. Edited by Howard Anderson, Philip B. Daghlian, and Irvin Ehrenpreis. Lawrence: University of Kansas Press, 1966.

Discusses the varied nature of Pope's correspondence; comments on the kaleidoscopic personality of Pope as seen through his letters; and suggests that Pope "helped to elevate letter-writing to an art, and he also helped to define and emphasize that art" (p. 36). See also 163.

654. Crittenden, Walter M. "The Letters of Alexander Pope," *Personalist*, XXXIX (1958), 38–47.

Reviews George Sherburn's edition of *The Correspondence of Alexander Pope* (see 670) and provides a biographical-interpretative account of Pope, through his correspondence.

655. Dearing, Vinton A. "The 1737 Editions of Alexander Pope's Letters," *Essays Critical and Historical Dedicated to Lily B. Campbell*. Berkeley and Los Angeles: University of California Press, 1950.

Comments on the order in which the 1737 editions were printed and investigates "the marked differences" in the contents of the editions. Dearing concludes that "the Robert's edition gives the earliest and best texts extant of no less than forty-three of Pope's letters" (p. 187) and that "none of Pope's editors," including Elwin and Courthope, "have produced the best texts" (p. 197) of Pope's correspondence.

656. ———. "Two Notes on the Copy for Pope's Letters. I. Pope's Use of Drafts of His Letters. II. An Example of Printing from Originals," *PBSA*, LI (1957), 327–33.

Discusses Pope's habit of sending transcripts to the press and examines the bibliographical significance of *Miscellanea* (1727), which contains twenty-five of Pope's letters to Henry Cromwell.

657. Dixon, Peter. "Pope and Steele," *N&Q*, CCX (1965), 451.

States that Pope's reference to a "modern writer," in a letter to William Trumbull, refers to Steele and paraphrases *Tatler*, no. 214.

658. Emden, Cecil S. "Alexander Pope: A Subject for Sym-

pathy," *Poets in Their Letters*. London: Oxford University Press, 1959.

Employing excerpts from Pope's correspondence, Emden maintains that Pope was "deceitful" in that he "tampered with the texts of his letters so as to make them reflect to his advantage when published" (p. 11) and that the poet was "insincere" because he pretended to be disdainful of fame, but that "many" of the letters do express Pope's genuine sentiments.

659. *Golliet, Jacques. "La Correspondance d'Alexander Pope," *EA*, XII (1959), 205–11.

660. Irving, William Henry. *The Providence of Wit in the English Letter Writers*. Durham, N.C.: Duke University Press, 1955.

Chapter six, "Pope and the Scriblerians," contains an analysis of Pope's "epistolary art." Irving examines Pope's use of models, the historical background of the composition and publication of Pope's correspondence, and Pope's attitudes toward writing letters.

661. *Letters of Alexander Pope*. Selected and with an introduction by John Butt. World's Classics, 574. London: Oxford University Press, 1960.

Prints the text of 206 letters written by Pope, which are based (with one exception) upon Sherburn's *Correspondence of Alexander Pope* (see 670). Butt explains that the selection made illustrates Pope's literary career, friendships, and nonliterary activities.

Reviewed by R. W. Zandvoort, *ES*, XLI (1960), 349; *TLS*, July 1, 1960, p. 420.

662. Link, Frederick M. "A New Pope Letter," *RES*, n.s., XV (1964), 398–99.

Provides the text of a Pope letter to the poet Thomson with a possible date of 1736.

663. Lunn, Alice Coyle. "Alexander Pope's Letters: The Image of a Good Man." Unpublished Ph.D. dissertation, Western Reserve University, 1967, *DA*, XXVIII (1967), 199A.

In uncovering the "aims and accomplishments" of Pope as a letter writer, Lunn defines the "definite relationship between Pope's correspondence and his poetical works and examines the historical, critical, and biographical implications" of Pope's letters.

664. Mack, Maynard. "Letters of Pope to Atterbury in the Tower," *RES*, XXI (1945), 117–25.

Explains the circumstances under which two letters written by Pope to Atterbury were actually ascribed to and published with the writings of the duke of Wharton. Mack also reproduces both letters and provides a "textual apparatus" in order to reveal "the kinds of suppression" (p. 121) which Pope made in the second letter.

665. Price, Cecil. "A Pope Letter," *TLS*, January 25, 1957, p. 49.

Describes a signed autograph letter catalogued by Puttick and Simpson in 1868 as a Pope letter to Mrs. Temple of Moor Park (see 672).

666. Rawson, C. J. "Some Unpublished Letters of Pope and Gay; and Some Manuscript Sources of Goldsmith's *Life of Thomas Parnell*," *RES*, n.s., X (1959), 371–87.

Examines ten transcripts of letters to Parnell from Pope and Gay, four of which are printed for the first time. Rawson states that the transcripts provide information on the Scriblerus Club and that they were probably utilized by Goldsmith for his *Life of Thomas Parnell*.

667. Rosenberg, Albert. "Date of John Gay's *An Epistle to Burlington*," *PQ*, XXX (1951), 94–96.

States that the correct dating of Gay's epistle is significant as it concerns Pope's correspondence. Rosenberg reveals that a Pope letter to Jervas which "mentions an attack on Blackmore by Gay in defense of Swift" (p. 95) establishes the fact that Gay's couplets attacking Blackmore are not part of Gay's epistle.

668. ———. "The Last Days of Sir Samuel Garth: A Footnote to a Pope Letter," *N&Q*, CCIV (1959), 272–74.

Quotes an excerpt from Pope's letter to Jervas in which

Pope defends Garth, cites "neglected information" concerning Garth, and interprets Pope's defense of Garth.

669. Rousseau, G. S. "A New Pope Letter," *PQ*, XLV (1966), 409–18.

Publishes the complete text (together with three plates) of a heretofore unattainable letter from Pope to Martha Blount. The letter's importance "lies in its revelation of Pope's aesthetic sensibilities, of his definitions of the *romantic,* and of his attitudes to painting and perspective at the time of composition of the *Epistle to Dr. Arbuthnot* and the *Imitations of Horace*" (p. 410).

670. Sherburn, George (ed.). *The Correspondence of Alexander Pope*. 5 vols. Oxford: Clarendon Press, 1956.

Contains over 2,100 letters in a single chronological series: volume I, 1704–1718; volume II, 1719–1728; volume III, 1729–1735; volume IV, 1736–1744; volume V, letters discovered too late to be included in the series. Sherburn includes an analytical index; an alphabetical list of the correspondences; annotations for names, places, allusions, and quotations; and footnotes which explain matters of style or variants. See also 306, 649, 652, 654, and 661.

Reviewed by Maynard Mack, *PQ*, XXXVI (1957), 389–99; William Frost, *YR*, XLVII (1957), 125–28; Robert W. Rogers, *JEGP*, LVI (1957), 615–19; Donald F. Bond, *MP*, LVI (1958), 55–59; Aubrey L. Williams, *RES*, n.s., IX (1958), 212–14; Richmond P. Bond, *MLR*, LIV (1959), 90–93.

671. ———. "Letters of Alexander Pope, Chiefly to Sir William Trumbull," *RES*, n.s., IX (1958), 388–406.

Publishes fourteen letters, "newly available," of Pope's correspondence with Trumbull, Ralph Bridges, Antony Englefield, and Elijah Fenton. Sherburn provides a list of all the Pope-Trumbull correspondence, explains the style of Pope's letters, and concludes that these new additions tend to enhance an understanding of Pope's formative years.

672. ———. "Mistaken Identity," *TLS*, February 22, 1957, p. 113.

Argues that the letter described by Cecil Price (see 665) "has no possible connection with Alexander Pope" since "it is not in his hand." Sherburn suggests that the writer was probably Elizabeth Temple's sister, Dorothy.

673. Wiley, Margaret Lee. "A Spence Letter," *English Studies in Honor of James Southall Wilson*. University of Virginia Studies, vol. IV. Charlottesville: University of Virginia, 1951.

> Provides a copy of a rough draft of a letter dated September 11, 1730, from Spence to Pope. Wiley states that the letter "with cancellation, revision, and marginal insertion" (p. 262) repudiates the assumption that all of the Spence-Pope correspondence was destroyed.

674. Wimsatt, William Kurtz, Jr. " 'Amicitiae Causa': A Birthday Present from Curll to Pope," *Restoration and Eighteenth-Century Literature. Essays in Honor of Alan Dugald McKillop*. Edited by Carroll Camden. Chicago: University of Chicago Press for William Marsh Rice University, 1963.

> Provides two plates: "Title-page medallion of Pope's *Letters*" and "Frontispiece of Curll's *New Letters of Mr. Pope*." The first is an engraved portrait done by Jonathan Richardson, while the second is "a carefully executed replica commissioned by . . . Edmond Curll." Wimsatt describes in detail the portraits and the history of their employment. See also 182.

ADDITIONAL FOREIGN CRITICISM

675.*Ehrenpreis, Irvin. "Orwell, Huxley, Pope," *Revue des Langues Vivantes,* XXIII (1957), 215–30.

676.*Fabian, Bernhard. "Popes Konzeption der 'Ruling Passion': eine Quellenuntersuchung," *Archiv,* CXCV (1959), 290–301.

677. *———. "Rückkehr zu Pope: eine Übersicht über die neueste Forschung," *Die neueren Sprachen,* 1957, pp. 300–314.

678. *Koppang, Ole. "En sammenlikning mellom Anthony Ashley Cooper, Earl of Shaftesbury og Alexander Pope," *Edda,* L (1950), 353–70.

679. *Lombardo, Agostino. "Osservazioni sulla poesia di Alexander Pope," *Letterature Moderne,* X (1960), 452–86.

680. *Praz, Mario. *La poesia di Pope e le sue origini.* Roma: Edizioni dell'Ateneo, 1962.

681. *Sanesi, Roberto. "Ancora Pope," *Aut Aut,* LXVII (1962), 72–73.

682. *Urner, Ursula. *Alexander Pope und die klassischlateinische Literatur.* Schweizer anglistische Arbeiten, no. 36. Bern: Francke Verlag, 1954.

INDEX

(References are to entry numbers.)

ABELARD, PETER, 350, 419
Adams, Percy G., 257
Addison, Joseph, 41, 230, 235, 364, 555
Adelsberger, Sister Agnes Stephen, 162
Aden, John M., 92, 258, 333, 334, 362, 420, 428, 493, 505
Adler, Jacob H., 259, 260, 335
Agate, James, 124
Allen, Ralph, 45
Allen, Robert J., 261
Allison, James, 125
Alpers, Paul J., 476
Altenbernd, A. Lynn, 477
Amarasinghe, Upali, 126
Ames, Alfred C., 127
Anderson, Howard, 163, 197, 198, 352, 653
Arbuthnot, John, 96, 496
Arlidge, Elizabeth, 648
Arnold, Matthew, 128
Art of Sinking in Poetry, 79, 82, 210, 291, 588, 605, 606, 610
Atkins, J. W. H., 75
Atterbury, Francis, 482, 594, 609, 664
Auden, W. H., 164
Audra, E., 1
Ault, Norman, 2, 37, 41, 165, 597
Avery, Emmett L., 363
Awad, Louis, 262

BAGNANI, GILBERT, 263
Baker, Donald C., 364
Balliet, Conrad A., 264
Banister (Pope's tutor), 608
Bate, W. Jackson, 274
Bateson, F. W., 3, 265, 287, 485
Battestin, Martin C., 93, 166
Baugh, Albert C., 240
Bawcutt, N. W., 535, 536
Bayley, John, 365
Beardsley, M. C., 161
Beaty, Frederick L., 94
Beaumont, Charles A., 421
Beck, Richard, 95, 167
Beers, Henry A., 168
Beljame, Alexandre, 169

Benét, William Rose, 42
Bentley, Richard, 506, 544
Berkeley, George, 191
Berland, Alwyn, 537
Berry, Francis, 266
Bibliography, 23–26
Biography, 13, 41–74, 164, 165, 169, 180, 190, 192, 205, 206, 208, 211, 222, 240, 246, 654, 663
Birch, Thomas, 89
Bishop, Carter R., 267
Blackmore, Sir Richard, 588, 667
Bladen, Martin, 575
Blanshard, Rufus A., 128, 170
Bloom, Harold, 61, 73, 209, 282
Bloom, Lillian D., 506
Bloomfield, Morton W., 538
Blount, Edward, 302
Blount, Martha, 37, 669
Blount, Teresa, 597
Bluestone, Max, 265, 268, 269, 313, 539
Blum, Margaret Morton, 171
Boccalini, Traiano, 580
Boddy, Margaret, 583
Boethius, 625
Boileau-Despréaux, Nicolas, 148, 272, 512, 532, 550, 572
Bolingbroke, Henry St. John, 423, 453
Bond, Donald F., 649
Bond, W. H., 6
Booth, Edward Townsend, 43
Borlase, Rev. William, 44
Bowles, W. L., 126
Boyce, Benjamin, 44, 45, 129, 270, 366, 422, 584, 585, 587, 612, 618
Boyette, Purvis E., 507
Boyle, Robert, 459
Boys, Richard C., 172
Bracher, Frederick, 46
Brady, Frank, 4
Bredenberg, Henrik N., Jr., 271
Bredvold, Louis I., 173
Brett, Reginald L., 423
Bridges, Ralph, 671
Brinton, Crane, 243
Brockbank, Philip, 5
Brooks, Benjamin Gilbert, 540

Brooks, Cleanth, 361, 367
Broome, William, 648
Brophy, Brigid, 368
Bross, Addison C., 508
Brower, Reuben Arthur, 6, 174, 175, 272, 513
Brown, Jack R., 369
Brown, Wallace Cable, 273, 494
Brownell, Morris Ruggles, 47
Brückmann, Patricia Laureen, 176, 370, 371
Brunner, Karl, 277
Brutus, 614, 617
Bryan, Robert A., 312
Bullitt, John, 274
Bullough, Geoffrey, 424
Burdon, William, 144
Burgess, C. F., 48, 96, 650
Burlington, Lady, 478
Burns, Robert, 94
Butler, Samuel, 384
Butt, John, 2, 7–9, 27, 28, 50, 177–80, 232, 478, 651, 652, 661
Byron, George Gordon, Lord, 128, 134, 147, 148, 216, 503
Bysshe, Edward, 623

CALLAN, NORMAN, 181, 619, 642
Camden, Carroll, 44, 175, 182, 221, 308, 533, 674
Cameron, Allen B., 425
Cameron, J. M., 179, 180, 336, 426
Cameron, W. J., 585
Campbell, Lily B., 655
Carew, Thomas, 485
Carlyle, Thomas, 149
Carnochan, W. B., 372
Carroll, John, 130
Cary, Walter, 230
Caryll, John, 589, 641
Case, Arthur Ellicott, 172
Castiglione, Baldassare, 349
Catesby, Thomas (Lord Paget), 160
Cave, Edward, 131
Cawley, A. C., 586
Cervantes, 549
Chambers, Jessie Rhodes, 541
Chandos, Duke of, 485
Chapin, Chester F., 542
Chapman, George, 631, 645
Chapman, R. W., 131

Chapple, J. A. V., 587
Character of Marlborough, 5
Chatman, Seymour, 275
Chaucer, Geoffrey, 315, 391, 413, 586, 590, 591, 602
Chesterfield, Lord, 137
Cheyne, Dr. George, 130
Churchill, Charles, 122, 494
Cibber, Colley, 25, 88, 140, 152, 156, 201, 269, 565, 566
Cicero, 349
Clark, David Ridgley, 620
Clark, Donald B., 132, 183
Clarke, Martin L., 621
Clifford, James L., 173, 184-86, 214, 217, 261, 295, 307, 342, 478, 551, 613, 651
Coleridge, Samuel T., 127, 128, 274, 340
Congleton, James Edmund, 316
Congreve, William, 387
Conington, John, 128
Connolly, Cyril, 509
Cook, Richard I., 373
Cooper, Anthony Ashley (earl of Shaftesbury), 233, 384, 678
Cope, Jackson I., 374
Copley, J., 375
Corneille, Pierre, 272
Coronation Epistle, 579, 598, 604
Correspondence (Pope's), 8, 52, 57, 62, 86, 89, 278, 302, 306, 427, 641, 648–74
Courthope, William J., 23, 476, 655
Cowler, Rosemary Elizabeth, 10, 653
Cowley, Abraham, 220, 327
Cowper, Judith, 37
Cowper, William, 75, 128, 151
Cox, Carrol Byron, Jr., 187
Crabbe, George, 145
Crawford, Charlotte E., 479
Criticism: additional foreign, 675–82; eighteenth- and nineteenth-century, 124–61; general criticism, 162–256
Crittenden, Walter M., 654
Cromwell, Henry, 278, 656
Cronin, Grover, Jr., 622
Crossett, John, 495
Crousaz, Jean-Pierre de, 131
Crowther, John W., 231, 543
Cruttwell, Patrick, 188, 427

Cunningham, Joseph S., 376
Curll, Edmund, 51, 131, 160, 552, 674
Curtis, Penelope, 189

DACIER, MADAME ANNE, 631, 638
Daghlian, Philip B., 163, 653
Daiches, David, 376
Dale, James, 97
Daniels, Elizabeth Adams, 480
Davenport, A., 377
Davies, Hugh S., 133
Davis, Herbert, 11
Davison, J. A., 544
Dearing, Vinton A., 29, 76, 655, 656
Deeney, John Joseph, S.J., 414
De Lisle, Harold F., 337
De Mordaunt, Walter J., 428
Deneau, Daniel P., 545
Denham, Sir John, 226
Dennis, John, 75, 129, 360
De Piles, Roger, 349
Derham, William, 455
De Selincourt, Aubrey, 190
De Stasio, Clotilde, 191
Discourse on Pastoral Poetry, 1, 10, 79, 83, 316, 370
Dixon, Peter, 276, 429, 496, 510, 511, 623, 624, 657
Dobrée, Bonamy, 49, 50, 169, 179, 180, 192, 430
Dobson, Austin, 149
Dodd, Betty Coshow, 497
Dolce, Lodovico, 349
Donaghey, Brian S., 625
Donne, John, 151, 220, 508, 519, 520, 534
Dorris, George E., 546
Dorset, Charles Sackville, earl of, 584, 585, 587
Douglas, Loyd, 588
Doyle, Paul A., 622
Drayton, Michael, 353
Dryden, John, 122, 126, 128, 150, 174, 175, 213, 217, 226, 257, 264, 272, 286, 292, 311, 328, 343, 357, 359, 384, 392, 398, 405, 494, 535, 574, 599, 602, 616
Dubos, Dr. René J., 480
Dunciad, 11, 19, 21, 22, 31, 34, 54, 82, 102, 106, 190, 192, 210, 211, 216, 222, 226, 236, 240, 241, 247, 269, 278, 288, 291, 296, 331, 361,
384, 388, 406, 512, 535–82, 614
Dupree, Robert Scott, 512
D'Urfey, Thomas, 78
Dyson, H. V. D., 50

EASTMAN, ARTHUR M., 193
Eckhoff, Lorentz, 277
Eddy, Donald D., 194
Editions, critical, 1–22, 419, 595, 610, 613
Edwards, Thomas (of Terrick), 484
Edwards, Thomas Robert, Jr., 195, 196, 278, 481, 513, 547, 548
Effross, Susi H., 98
Ehrenpreis, Irvin, 163, 197, 653, 675
Elegy to the Memory of an Unfortunate Lady, 210, 229, 592, 601
Eliot, T. S., 102, 107, 115, 120
Elledge, Scott, 77
Ellis, William D., Jr., 78
Eloisa to Abelard, 68, 98, 210, 216, 271, 296, 308, 414–19
Elwin, Rev. Whitwell, 12, 57, 655
Elzevir edition of Horace, 514
Emden, Cecil S., 658
Empson, William, 338
Englefield, Antony, 671
Epilogue to the Satires. See Satires
Epistle to Dr. Arbuthnot, 27, 113, 118, 211, 273, 282, 291, 343, 441, 493–504, 509, 515, 523, 537, 669
Epistle to Harley, 306, 613
Epistles of Horace Imitated. See Satires
Erasmus, 549
Erdman, David V., 134
Erskine-Hill, Howard H., 482, 483, 549, 589
Essay on Criticism, 22, 24, 75, 79, 83, 94, 95, 108, 112, 114, 119, 145, 190, 192, 222, 226, 227, 236, 241, 245, 265, 269, 271, 296, 298, 313, 328, 333–61, 370.
Essay on Man, 4, 11, 14, 17, 21, 22, 31, 36, 42, 68, 95, 99–101, 107, 108, 115, 116, 139, 154, 159, 192, 222, 229, 233, 236, 241, 246, 247, 273, 278, 288, 291, 296, 298, 301, 310, 321, 335, 420–75, 570, 614
Ethic Epistles. See Moral Essays

Eusden, Laurence, 490
Eustathius, 635, 638

FABIAN, BERNHARD, 99, 431–33, 626, 676, 677
Fairclough, G. Thomas, 550
Faley, Brother Roland, 434
Fanshawe, Richard, 86, 517
Farewell to London, 563
Feder, Lillian, 198
Felps, Jettie Irving, 199
Fenner, Arthur, Jr., 339
Fenton, Elijah, 671
Field, P. J., 378
Fielding, Henry, 93, 155, 166, 573
Fineman, Daniel A., 135, 590
Fleischmann, Wolfgang Bernard, 435, 498
Florio, John, 377
Fogle, Richard Harter, 340
Forcione, Alban, 100
Ford, Boris, 181
Forseth, Roger Daniels, 279
Forster, E. M., 325
Fortesque, William, 29, 35
Foxon, David F., 30, 31, 436
Fraser, Russell A., 437
Friedman, Arthur, 551
Frost, William, 200, 379, 438, 627
Fry, John, 151
Frye, Northrop, 356
Fuller, John, 591
Fussell, Paul, 280

GARDINER, JAMES, 81
Garth, Sir Samuel, 373, 668
Gay, John, 28, 34, 35, 51, 78, 89, 96, 273, 591, 650, 666, 667
Gelli, Giovanni Battista, 432
George II, 521
Gilbert, Vedder M., 431, 484
Gildon, Charles, 138, 366, 564
Gillie, Christopher, 592
Gilmore, Thomas B., 201
Goethe, Johann Wolfgang von, 99
Goggin, L. P., 380
Goldberg, S. L., 202
Golden, Samual A., 381
Goldgar, Bertrand A., 79, 439
Goldstein, Malcolm, 80, 628
Göller, Karl Heinz, 281
Golliet, Jacques, 659
Gosse, Edmund, 149

Grabes, Herbert, 440
Graves, Robert, 203
Gray, Thomas, 97, 103, 111, 118, 197, 451
Greany, Helen T., 101, 204
Green-Armytage, A. H. N., 382
Greene, Donald J., 282, 441
Gregory the Great, 350
Gregory, Horace, 205
Grierson, Herbert J. C., 206
Griffith, Reginald Harvey, 23, 24, 81, 552, 553, 610
Guardian, 10, 34, 77, 79, 191, 254, 316, 588, 590
Guarini, Giambattista, 85, 86
Guerinot, Joseph V., 32
Gustafson, Richard Clarence, 629

HAGEDORN, RALPH, 24, 514
Hagstrum, Jean H., 283
Hall, Bishop Joseph, 495
Halsband, Robert, 51, 52, 207
Hambrick, Thomas Gregory, 515
Hamm, Victor M., 341
Hardy, John, 136
Harley, Edward (earl of Oxford), 499, 613, 650
Harrison, G. B., 208
Hart, James D., 442
Hart, Jeffrey P., 102, 137
Hart, John Forest, 443
Harte, Walter, 81
Hauser, David R., 317, 554
Hays, Charles, 575
Hazlitt, William, 128
Heath-Stubbs, John, 13
Heinsius, Nicholas, 506
Heloise, 419
Henderson, Anthony Gordon, 53
Herrick, Robert, 485
Herring, George Dewitt, 284
Hervey, Lord John, 156, 166, 497, 500, 501
Hibbard, G. R., 485
Highet, Gilbert, 54
Hilles, Frederick W., 61, 73, 209, 282
Hilty, Peter Daniel, 318
Hogarth, William, 106
Homer, 9, 11, 15, 52, 128, 135, 155, 169, 192, 236, 240, 245, 272, 492, 574, 621, 626, 629, 634, 636, 637, 645, 647

Honoré, Jean, 138
Hooker, Edward Niles, 285, 342
Hopkins, Robert H., 555, 593
Horace, 7, 92, 128, 245, 272, 379, 476, 479, 505, 506, 512, 515, 516, 518, 523, 528
Howard, Leon, 139
Hughes, John, 419
Hughes, Richard Edward, 286, 444, 516
Hume, David, 112
Hunt, Leigh, 124
Hunt, Percival, 289
Hunter, G. K., 517, 518
Hunting, Robert S., 594, 609
Huseboe, Arthur Robert, 82, 210
Hussey, Richard, 630–33
Hutchens, Eleanor N., 103
Huxley, Aldous, 675
Hyman, Stanley Edgar, 383
Hynes, Samuel L., 83

Iliad, translation, 6, 15, 111, 121, 127, 135, 155, 169, 190, 192, 236, 240, 245, 283, 379, 441, 619–22, 626, 627, 629–34, 636–38, 640–42
Iliad, Preface, 77, 79, 347
Imitations of Horace. See Satires
Irving, William Henry, 660

JACK, IAN, 211, 384, 519
Jackson, James L., 385
Jacobs, Elijah L., 55
James, G. Ingli, 287
Jefferson, D. W., 179, 180
Jernigan, Jack Julian, 288
Jervas, Charles 42, 261, 667, 668
Johnson, Carol Holmes, 556, 557
Johnson, Charles, 158
Johnson, James William, 212
Johnson, Samuel, 75, 92, 114, 125, 128, 129, 131, 146, 303, 494
Johnson, T., 24
Johnston, Arthur, 213
Johnston, Elizabeth, 289
Jones, Evan, 520
Jones, H. W., 343
Jones, John A., 290
Jones, Richard Foster, 214, 215, 239
Jones, William Powell, 140, 445, 446
Jonson, Ben, 474, 485
Julow, Victor, 386

Junius, Franciscus, 349
Jurgens, Heather, 319
Justinian, Emperor, 527
Juvenal, 92, 398, 505

KALLICH, MARTIN, 344, 345, 447–52
Kalmey, Robert P., 415
Keats, John, 365
Kenner, Hugh, 558
Kent, William, 63
Kerby-Miller, Charles, 595, 596
Kernan, Alvin B., 291, 559
Kiehl, James W., 320
King, Archbishop William, 458
Kinghorn, A. M., 141
Kinsely, J., 142
Kishler, Thomas C., 104
Kliger, Samuel, 346
Knight, Douglas, 634–37
Knight, G. Wilson, 216, 476
Koppang, Ole, 678
Korninger, Siegfried, 277
Korte, Donald M., 105
Koziol, Herbert, 387
Krieger, Murray, 388
Kronenberger, Louis, 56, 57
Krutch, Joseph Wood, 217

LAIRD, JOHN, 453
Lamartine, Alphonse, 109
Landa, Louis A., 173, 186, 214, 217, 261, 295, 478, 551, 613
Lauter, Paul, 389
Law, Edmund, 458
Lawlor, Nancy K., 454
Lawrence, D. H., 115
Leach, Frederick D., 106
Leavis, F. R., 292, 560
Le Bossu, René, 16, 588
Lee, Jae Ho, 107
Leedy, Paul F., 143
Leibniz, Gottfried Wilhelm, 462
Le Page, R. B., 293
Lessing, Gotthold, 99, 463
Levine, Jay Arnold, 218, 486, 521
Lewis, David Earle, 58
Lewis, Sinclair, 104
Link, Frederick M., 662
Lintot, Bernard, 24, 165, 169
Litz, Francis E., 108, 455
Locke, John, 470, 471
Lomazzo, 349
Lombard, C. M., 109

Lombardo, Agostino, 679
Loomis, Emerson Robert, 144
Lorimer, E. O., 169
Lorimer, H. L., 635, 638
Lovejoy, A. O., 354
Lowell, James Russell, 150
Lucretius, 435
Lunn, Alice Coyle, 663
Lynch, Harry, 59
Lyttelton, George, 614

MABBOTT, THOMAS O., 145, 487
McAleer, John J., 639
Macauley, Thomas, 149
MacDonald, Wilbert Lorne, 60, 146
Mace, Dean Tolle, 347
Mack, Maynard, 14–16, 33, 34, 36,
    41, 61, 174, 187, 208, 219–21, 265,
    287, 292, 294, 295, 321, 349, 426,
    469, 485, 499, 573, 664
Mackenzie, M. L., 390
McKillop, Alan Dugald, 44, 175,
    182, 221, 222, 308, 533, 596, 674
Macklem, Michael, 456
MacLaine, Allan H., 110
McLeod, A. L., 28, 35
MacLure, Millar, 223, 462
MacSwiny, Owen, 422
Maffei, Scipione, 546
Mahaffey, Lois Kathleen, 62, 224
Mahoney, John L., 147
Malarkey, Stoddard, 391
Malebranche, Nicolas, 341
Malins, Edward, 63
Mandel, Barrett J., 416
Mandeville, Bernard, 233, 476
Manley, Francis, 457
Manuscripts, 27–40, 330, 355, 491,
    603
Maresca, Thomas E., 522, 523
Marlowe, Christopher, 362
Marmion, Shakerly, 374
Marriot, Betty, 597
Marsh, Robert, 471
Marshall, Robert Carlisle, 561
Marshall, William H., 148
Marvell, Andrew, 220, 378, 485
Mathias, Thomas J., 144
Maud, Ralph N., 597, 598
Maxwell, J. C., 111–14, 225, 322,
    357, 500, 562, 563, 599
Mead, G. C. F., 600
Meagher, John C., 501

Means, James A., 226, 348
Medford, Floyd, 458
Melchiori, Giorgio, 323
Mell, Donald Charles, Jr., 601
Meller, Horst, 627, 646
Melmoth, William, 622
Melville, Herman, 113
Memoirs of the Extraordinary Life,
    Works, and Discoveries of Marti-
    nus Scriblerus, 34, 75, 156, 595,
    596
Mendelssohn, Moses, 463
Mengel, Elias F., Jr., 502
Messiah, 1, 245, 271, 611
Meynell, Alice, 116
Midgley, E. G., 524
Miller, John H., 227
Milton, John, 91, 167, 272, 322,
    367, 402, 411, 472, 582
Monk, Samuel Holt, 197, 198, 228,
    349, 352, 459
Montagu, Lady Mary Wortley, 51,
    52, 54, 55, 58, 62, 484
Montague, Gene B., 149
Montaigne, Michel de, 529
Moore, Frank Harper, 392
Moore, John Robert, 64, 324, 564
Moral Essays, 21, 40, 75, 82, 131,
    210, 216, 233, 236, 240, 247, 273,
    278, 288, 306, 312, 321, 430, 443,
    476–92, 555, 570
Moran, Berna, 460
Moritz, Karl Philipp, 99
Morris, Alton C., 312
Morris, E. E., 17
Morse, J. Mitchell, 350
Moskovit, Leonard Adolph, 525, 526
Mudrick, Marvin, 602
Murphree, A. A., 312
Murray, Byron D., 150

NEWTON, FRANCES J., 115
Newton, Sir Isaac, 445, 446, 475
Nichols, John, 39
Nierenberg, Edwin H., 229, 325
Nixon, Howard Kenneth, Jr., 84

O'CASEY, SEAN, 101
Odyssey, 10, 16, 77, 79, 91, 236, 397
Ogilby, John, 631
Ogle, George, 510
O'Hehir, Brendan P., 326, 417
Oliver, John, 600

Oliver, Leslie M., 327
Oliver, Dr. William, 44
On the Death of the Queen and Marshal Luxembourg, 584, 585, 587, 612
Orwell, George, 675
Osborn, James M., 65, 72, 230, 527
Ovid, 272, 562
Oxford, Edward Harley, earl of, 499, 613, 650

PAFFORD, J. H. P., 151
Paget, Thomas Catesby, Lord, 168
Parkin, Rebecca Price, 296–98, 393, 394, 488
Parnell, Thomas, 613, 666
Pastorals, 85, 190, 233, 245, 271, 273, 278, 296, 316, 318, 323, 328, 331, 370, 590
Patten, Faith Harris, 299
Peacock, Thomas Love, 382
Peavy, Charles Druery, III, 25, 565
Peers, E. Allison, 98
Perella, Nicolas J., 85, 86
Peri Bathous, 79, 82, 210, 291, 588, 605, 606, 610
Persius, 505
Peterson, William M., 152
Petit, Herbert H., 231, 543
Pettit, Henry, 351, 418
Philips, Ambrose, 78, 316, 490
Phillipson, John S., 395
Pinkus, Philip, 566, 567
Piozzi, Hester Thrale, 274
Pittermann, Erwein, 528
Pittock, Joan, 153
Pittock, Malcolm, 396
Pliny the Elder, 349
Ploch, Richard A., 397
Poirier, Richard, 513
Pollard, Arthur, 398, 461
Pope, Alexander: allusion (use of), 183, 272, 295, 334, 376, 402, 410, 414, 545, 547, 554, 575, 578; ambiguity (use of), 288, 336, 354; antithesis (use of), 345, 447, 452; as a critic, 75–91; as a translator and editor, 618–47; deism, 160, 454, 551; diction, 22, 164, 195, 216, 249, 260, 262, 263, 276, 279, 284, 306, 307, 309, 310, 403, 447, 479, 557, 592, 613, 616; drama (interest in), 210, 267;

humor (use of), 297, 298; imagery (use of), 183, 249, 261, 265, 268, 269, 271, 278–80, 295, 297, 299, 300, 310, 313, 320, 340, 344, 351, 367, 372, 376, 395, 411, 414, 447, 450, 475, 502, 533, 539, 541, 547, 561, 573; influence in America, 139, 159, 442; influence in France, 98, 100, 463; influence in Germany, 99, 463; influence in Iceland, 95; influence in Italy, 132; influence in Spain, 98, 100; irony (use of), 22, 297, 376, 399, 414, 457, 521, 559; nature (concept of), 162, 195, 239, 249, 309, 325, 333, 334, 336, 354, 361, 423, 469; prosody, 18, 257, 259, 260, 264, 275, 309, 310, 312, 334, 335, 376, 520, 561; satire (use of), 22, 67, 87, 193, 198, 204, 258, 267, 283, 284, 291, 292, 373, 521–23, 526, 550, 570, 576, 610; Twickenham (garden and/or grotto), 44, 46, 47, 53, 59, 61, 63, 64, 221, 477; wit, 18, 22, 67, 292, 295, 333, 338, 342, 355, 361
Porláksson, Jón, 167
Potter, George R., 232
Pottle, Frederick A., 61, 73, 209, 282
Potts, Abbie Findlay, 568
Poussin, Nicolas, 323
Powell, Dilys, 67
Praz, Mario, 680
Preston, John, 399
Price, Cecil, 665, 672
Price, Frances, 116
Price, Martin, 233, 234
Priestley, F. E. L., 462
Prior, Matthew, 68, 498, 504, 535
Procopius, 527
Provost, Foster, 328
Puttick and Simpson, 665
Pyle, Fitzroy, 400

QUEEN ANNE, 381
Quennell, Peter, 18, 205
Quintana, Ricardo, 401
Quintillian, 349

RABELAIS, FRANCOIS, 549
Racine, Jean Baptiste, 272
Ramsey, Paul, 352

Ransom, John Crowe, 428
Rape of the Lock, 11, 20, 22, 97, 103, 104, 110, 118, 120, 190, 192, 210, 211, 216, 222, 227, 233, 236, 240, 241, 271, 274, 278, 283, 288, 296, 298, 331, 362–413, 542, 549, 567
Rapin, René, 81, 328, 349
Rawlinson, David H., 235
Rawson, C. J., 503, 529, 666
Reaves, R. B., Jr., 117
Reichard, Hugo M., 87, 402, 530, 569
Richard of Saint Victor, 350
Richardson, Jonathan, 674
Richardson, Samuel, 130
Ricks, Christopher, 531
Riggs, E. S., 353
Riling, Mildred, 403, 408
Ripa, Cesare, 349
Rippy, Frances Mayhew, 68
Roberts, Mark, 118
Robertson, C. A., 312
Robertson, D. A., Jr., 315
Rochester, earl of, 615
Rogal, Samuel J., 88
Rogers, Robert W., 463–65, 570, 603
Root, Robert, Kilburn, 236
Roscoe, William, 126
Rosenberg, Albert, 667, 668
Røstvig, Maren-Sofie, 237
Rousseau, G. S., 640, 669
Ruffhead, William, 60, 69, 146, 154
Ruhe, E. L., 89
Russell, Leonard, 67
Ryley, Robert Michael, 69, 154, 604
Ryskamp, Charles, 641

Sackett, S. J., 155, 605
Sackville, Charles (earl of Dorset), 584, 585, 587
Saintsbury, George, 149
St. Vincent, Edwin Harold, 300
Sambrook, A. J., 156, 571
Sanders, Charles, 354
Sanesi, Roberto, 681
Satires, 7, 21, 30, 33, 40, 68, 92, 151, 233, 240, 245, 269, 275, 282, 291, 298, 312, 394, 443, 499, 505–34, 555, 570, 669
Satires of Dr. John Donne . . . Versified. See Satires

Say, Samuel, 127
Schafer, Robert G., 489
Schlüter, Kurt, 329
Schmitz, Robert M., 37, 330, 355, 642
Schonhorn, Manuel R., 404, 490
Scott, Sir Walter, 39
Scriblerus Club, 595, 607, 666
Scriblerus, Martinus. *See Memoirs of . . . Martinus Scriblerus*
Seamon, Roger G., 606
Sebeok, Thomas A., 275
Secord, Arthur W., 238
Seed, Jeremiah, 108
Sen, Sailendra Kumar, 157, 643
Seronsy, Cecil C., 405
Settle, Elkanah, 490
Sewell, George, 225
Shaftesbury, Anthony Ashley Cooper, earl of, 233, 384, 467, 678
Shakespeare, William, 225, 240, 402, 437, 535, 568, 618, 624, 628, 639, 643
Shakespeare, Pope's edition of, 10, 75, 77, 79, 225, 240, 618, 623, 624, 628, 639, 643, 644
Shaver, Chester L., 119
Shea, John S., 197, 198, 352
Sheffield, John, 628
Shelley, Percy Bysshe, 110
Sherbo, Arthur, 572
Sherburn, George, 38, 39, 70, 71, 173, 186, 214, 217, 239, 240, 295, 301, 478, 551, 573, 607, 613, 649, 652, 654, 661, 670–72
Shiels, Robert, 129
Shudofsky, Maurice M., 158
Shugrue, Michael, 608
Sibley, Agnes Marie, 159
Siegrist, Ottmar K., 302
Simon, Irène, 120, 241, 466, 467
Simpson, Puttick and, 665
Sitwell, Edith, 57
Skelton, Robin, 179, 180
Skerrett, Maria (Molly), 62, 527
Smith, A. J. M., 356
Smith, Constance I., 357, 574
Smith, David Nichol, 178, 301, 644
Smith, J. C., 206
Smollett, Tobias, 105
Sparrow, John, 468, 609
Speaight, George, 121

Spector, Robert Donald, 160
Spence, Joseph, 33, 65, 72, 77, 84, 673
Spenser, Edmund, 272, 498
Sprat, Thomas, 384
Stanley, E. G., 303
Starrett, Agnes Lynch, 289
Statius, 608
Steele, Richard, 593, 657
Steensma, Robert C., 242
Steevens, George, 392
Steeves, Edna Leake, 610
Stein, William Bysshe, 358
Stephen, Sir Leslie, 243
Sterne, Laurence, 94
Stiker, J. M., 575
Stockdale, Percival, 136
Suckling, Sir John, 524
Sühnel, Rudolf, 627, 645, 646
Sullivan, J. P., 90
Surtz, Edward L., 611
Sutherland, James R., 19, 244, 406, 540, 576
Sutherland, W. O. S., Jr., 407
Swift, Jonathan, 38, 39, 96, 130, 138, 173, 204, 236, 242, 531, 610, 667
Sypher, Wylie, 304, 305

TANNER, TONY, 577
Tate, Allen, 171
Temple of Fame, 192, 216, 278, 283, 394, 586
Temple sisters, 665, 672
Tennyson, Alfred, 123
Theobald, Lewis, 76, 269, 576
Theocritus, 272
Theodora, Empress, 527
Thomson, James, 117, 662
Thomson, James A. K., 245
Thornton, Francis Beauchesne, 246
Thorpe, James, 91
Thrale (Piozzi), Hester, 274
Three Hours after Marriage, 80, 152
Tickell, Thomas, 619
Tillotson, Geoffrey, 20, 127, 247–49, 306–10, 336, 398, 403, 408, 532, 612, 613
Tobin, James Edward, 26, 250
Todd, William B., 30, 40
Tonson, Jacob, 169
Torchiana, Donald T., 614

Trickett, Rachel, 251
Troy, Frederick S., 469
Trumbull, Sir William, 71, 625, 657, 671
Tuveson, Ernest, 470, 471

Universal Prayer, 95, 109, 603
Urner, Ursula, 682

VALDÉS, MELÉNDEZ, 100
Vandeput, Lady Frances, 135
Varenius, Bernhardus, 596
Vasari, Giorgio, 349
Vaughan, Thomas, 460
Vieth, David M., 578, 579, 615
View of London and Westminster, 536, 581
Villars, Abbé Nicolas de, 371, 397
Virgil, 213, 245, 255, 272, 322, 326, 328, 402
Voltaire, 380

WAIN, JOHN, 252, 592
Wallace, Joel Wise, 409
Waller, Edmund, 226, 524
Walpole, Robert, 93, 224, 527
Walsh, William, 86
Warburton, William, 42, 69, 129, 154, 160, 465, 527, 562
Warren, Austin, 187, 331
Warton, Joseph, 69, 75, 77, 125, 126, 128, 129, 136, 142, 143, 146, 153, 157, 161, 168, 572, 588
Warton, Thomas, 141
Wasser, Henry, 472
Wasserman, Earl R., 220, 253, 332, 410, 481, 491, 616
Watson, George, 359
Watson, Melvin R., 254
Watt, F. W., 223, 462
Weatherly, Edward H., 122
Weinbrot, Howard D., 311, 504
Wellington, James E., 21, 255, 419, 492
Welsted, Leonard, 32, 135
West, Richard, 97
Wharton, Philip, 664
Wiley, Margaret Lee, 673
Wilkins, A. N., 360
William III, 324
Williams, Aubrey L., 1, 265, 268, 312, 313, 411, 533, 536, 580–82
Williams, Charles, 314

Williams, Edward Kneale, 473
Williams, T. G., 256
Wilson, Edmund, 123
Wilson, James Southall, 673
Wimsatt, William Kurtz, Jr., 22,
 73, 74, 161, 315, 361, 412, 674
Winchilsea, Lady Anne Finch, 459,
 535
Windsor Forest, 117, 192, 211, 216,
 227, 271, 273, 308, 317, 320–22,
 324–30, 332, 365, 370
Woodhouse, A. S. P., 223, 462

Wordsworth, William, 119, 128,
 274, 279, 318, 568
Works (1717), 1, 10, 29, 34, 79
Wronker, Stanley S., 474
Wycherley, William, 76, 102, 343

YOUNG, EDWARD, 479, 648

ZIMMERMANN, HANS-JOACHIM, 534,
 617, 627, 646, 647
Zoellner, Robert H., 420, 428, 475
Zucker, David H., 413